GOD'S
Faithfulness

Wayne Bedeau

GOD'S FAITHFULNESS

Copyright © 2022 Wayne Bedeau.

All rights reserved. No part of this book may be used or reproduced by any means, graphic, electronic, or mechanical, including photocopying, recording, taping or by any information storage retrieval system without the written permission of the author except in the case of brief quotations embodied in critical articles and reviews.

Because of the dynamic nature of the Internet, any web addresses or links contained in this book may have changed since publication and may no longer be valid. The views expressed in this work are solely those of the author and do not necessarily reflect the views of the publisher, and the publisher hereby disclaims any responsibility for them.

ISBN: 978-9-7682-9027-4 (sc)

Print information available on the last page.

Contents

Preface v

Acknowledgments vii

Dedication ix

The Purpose In Living... 1

In Search of Me... 11

Changed Life 18

Meeting My Bride... 23

Losing our home!.. 41

Family Matters.. 58

Preface

I am *WAYNE BEDEAU*. It is approximately 10:48 p.m. on April 18, 2007. That makes me forty-eight years and fourteen days old as I commence this autobiography.

I consider this a long overdue, great moment in my life. I feel pressed by the Lord to document the many events he has used over the years to shape my life in a book. I trust this book will not just be a blessing to you as you read it but will also bring you great joy and deliverance.

Acknowledgments

First and foremost, I give thanks to Almighty God who is the Lord of my Life, the Author and Finisher of my Faith and the Holy Spirit who is my Guide and Comforter. I thank my wife, Pastor Agatha Ann Bedeau, for being my biggest supporter for one year shy of four decades of marriage and my four beautiful children: Dwayne, Pastor Swayne, Rachel Bedeau Daniels and Joshua Bedeau. Thanks to Apostle Trevor Joefield for his encouragement to write and edit the book and Apostle Terrence Honore for doing the second part of editing and making the connections with the publisher. I thank Apostle Dr. Mark Daniel for his contribution in making this happen. Thanks to my nephew Dareem Scipio for his help with the editing. Bishop Steve Belgrove, Apostle Desmond John, Pastor Dexter Downes, Pastor Eric and Arlene Joseph, Pastor Rajkumar Balkissoon, Pastor Ram Roopnarine, Prophet Trevor Grant and my sisters, thank you. Wendy Authur Lopez and my daughter Rachel Bedeau Daniels, I appreciate your financial aid. Not forgetting the brethren from Brooklyn, New York—thank you. My former co-worker for the encouragement to write and my brother from another Mother, Pastor Gary Pollard, you have my deepest gratitude.

Dedication

This book is dedicated to my parents: Robert John Bedeau and Eugenia Leah Bedeau (fondly called 'TANTY'). I was trusting God that my Mom would have been alive to see the completion and launching of this book but unfortunately, God called her home in the year 2020 at the age of eighty-eight. My dad went to be with the Lord in 2016 at the age of ninety. These two remained stalwart in their unwavering love for me when I needed it most. They stood with me through the good times and the bad times. Even though I was a bit stubborn, they never gave up on me.

The Purpose In Living

I was born on Mon Chagrin Street, San Fernando Trinidad, to the most loving father, Mr. Robert John Bedeau and wonderful mother Ms. Leah Bedeau, formerly known as Speedwell. My dad was born in Carriacou, Grenada, and my mom was born at Brothers Road, Trinidad. I'm the only boy amongst six children and I count it an honour to be a part of my family. My parents mentioned they were hoping for another boy though, as my dad loved boy children, to carry on the family name. However, I believe it is the will of God that I am alive today to fulfil and declare his works.

I once questioned my mother about their decision to move from San Fernando. She informed me that the change was due to them living in a rental situation and their need to get out of such. This led to my maternal uncle locating a house in another village, where we eventually resided as house owners. My parents bought the house and we moved into a new home in the year 1964. I was four years old and couldn't fully understand the situation at the time. However, I can now safely say, *I believe it was the will of God.*

When my parents moved to the new area, we were a family of six—my mom and dad, and four kids: my eldest sister Brenda, my second eldest sister Annie, then Bernadette and myself. While there, we welcomed two more sisters: Simonette and my baby sister Cheryl. Allow me to interject that at times we may not understand God's plan and will for our lives, but, as the scriptures say, *"For I know the thoughts and plans that I have for you, says the Lord, thoughts, and plans for welfare and peace and not for evil, to give you hope in your final outcome,"* **Jeremiah 29:11 (AMP).** I have now come to understand everything that happens in our lives, be it negative or positive, is preparing us for where God is taking us. As Jeremiah says, **"...to give you hope in your _final outcome_."** In other words, whatever happens to you, there is still hope for you, so, never give up.

I attended the Roman Catholic School until standard seven, a Technical Institute for about two years, and St. Kevin's College for a short period. I would describe my school years as exciting; especially those spent in primary school. In school, I was a cool and quiet guy, not rude nor disobedient to my teachers, and was willing to learn. My teachers were willing to assist me in my learning experience which enabled me to excel. I loved English Language very much and will never forget one teacher giving me a scolding (not abuse) and telling me, "It was all for you to learn your work and excel just like everybody else." I must say though, *I believe it is important that children be disciplined in school.* The bible says, **"The rod and reproof give wisdom: but a child left to himself bringeth his mother shame... Correct thy son and he shall give thee rest; yea, he shall give delight unto thy soul." Proverbs 29:15, 17 (KJV).**

GOD knew the nature man was born with makes it impossible for him or her to do right. The bible also says, **"Foolishness is bound in the heart of a child, but the rod of correction shall drive it far from him." Proverbs 22:15 (KJV).** I'm not saying that if corporal punishment were reinstated in the school system that violence would stop, but rather, everyone needs to do their part to produce a changed society. The Pastor, Evangelist, Prophet, Priest, Lawyer, Doctor, Magistrate, Basketball Player, Footballer, the man on the street, the Government Senator, the Opposition Senator, even a mother and a father must do his or her part to create a better society. In fact, everyone in a society must take it upon themselves to contribute to its change. I also believe we must reach the stage where if we see each other engaged in wrongdoing, we will gather the will and the strength to stop speaking negative things over our nation and each other and speak into the situation the positive we want to see happen instead. The Bible says, **"Death and life are in the power of the tongue: and they that love it shall eat the fruit thereof." Proverbs 18:21 (KJV).**

Joshua made a decision on behalf of his family that's recorded in Joshua 24:15. Even though some of the Israelites were serving the gods of the Amorites, Joshua took a just, bold, firm, and brave decision to speak on behalf of his house. He said, *"...but as for me and my house we will serve the LORD."* **Joshua 24:15b (KJV)**. The conclusion of the matter is; if we want a change, we must speak change, walk change, and act change. Even when we are not seeing change, we should speak it—in our homes, over our children, over our marriages, over our government, over our justice system, over our jobs, and even over our young people. Speak it in the morning, noontime, in the evening when we go to sleep, in the middle of the night, and even when we wake. We must continue to speak change. We have to also believe what we speak, *"For with the heart man believeth unto righteousness; and with the mouth, confession is made unto salvation."* **Romans 10:10 (KJV)**.

I was unsuccessful at the Common Entrance Examination, but I believe that passing through the school system afforded me a fair knowledge of right and wrong. This was in addition to the training I received from my parents.

I remember a period of my life when I suffered from a rare sickness. I suffered with uncontrollable bowel movement. It was so severe that I would have bowel movements and not even know it. Yes, it was that troubling. My illness reached the stage where I had to wear a cloth diaper below my school pants to attend school, and I also had to do my own laundry. That was one of the most embarrassing periods of my life! I remember the school children calling me, "too-too boy." I would not like anyone to go through that experience. I can say today, *Thank God for praying parents. Even though they were not totally surrendered to the Lord at that time, GOD answered their prayers on my behalf.*

I remember my mom taking me to different doctors, spending money on medication but to no avail. After no results from the medical doctors, my parents took me to self-proclaimed doctors also known as witchcraft doctors. We were given all kinds of frivolous explanations for my condition. One witchcraft doctor scared me to death! He told my mom that someone had thrown and buried something in our yard. It was thrown for my parents, but I stepped on it first; that's why I was in that condition. He also said that he needed to come to our home and dig up what was buried in the yard. The part that scared me to death, was when he said, there is an evil spirit that would someday come back for me. I knew then, he was talking about death, and I feared that I would die anytime. My life was a nightmare after hearing that statement. I can't remember how old I was, but I was old enough to know that my days were numbered! You have to forgive me; I did not know God the way I know Him now. So, I believed what I heard and was waiting for that fateful day. I didn't know that my mom was praying like Hannah from the bible. She got up one morning and gave my father the last money she had and told him to bring her a bottle of Robert Cough Syrup. Dad did not hesitate nor even oppose but obliged and brought the bottle of Robert Cough Syrup that evening. Mom gave it to me to drink and within the space of three days I was completely healed; diarrhoea ceased completely.

Incidentally, my father's first name is Robert. I don't know what the connection between dad's name and mom's dream was. In mom's dream, someone came and told her to give me Robert Cough Syrup. She took note that it was not Imodium, Lomotil, flour and soda water nor even guava bud, for those were the medications that would normally be used for diarrhoea. However, it was Robert Cough Syrup. The first thought was that this is medicine for the common cold. But we serve a God who has chosen the foolish things of the world to confound the wise. **1 Corinthians 1:27 (KJV)** A lot of medications were given to me: egg and aloes, egg and orange juice, and many more. I consumed all of them because I wanted to be healed. I give God a high note of praise today for healing me when He did and the way He did. I highlighted Robert Cough Syrup but I know now it was not Robert Cough Syrup but God. He is God all by Himself, and of whom it is recorded in His Word. In **Isaiah 53:5 (KJV)** it says, *"But he was wounded for our transgressions, he was bruised for our iniquities: the chastisement of our peace was upon him; and with his stripes we are healed."*

My being alive today is all because of God's healing power! If it wasn't for Him, I don't know where I would have been today. As the songwriter says, "I don't know why JESUS Loves Me, I don't know why he cares, I don't know why He sacrificed His life, but thank God, He did." He loves us with an everlasting love that has no bounds nor limits; it goes beyond the highest heights and reaches to the lowest depth.

You may be going through what you consider to be the worst time of your life at present, but I want you to know that God really, really, loves you. You may not realize that, but think about the things you've been going through to knock you off your feet. I mean, you have been literally knocked over flat on your back, and when you tell yourself, "this is it," you are on your feet again. It is because of God's Love for you, you are what you are today. People may have forsaken you, your husband, wife, children, or best friends may have given up on you, folks you thought would always be there for you may have even turned their backs on you. However, as you look back today, you would realize that God's love never gave up on you.

"For God so loved the world, that he gave his only begotten Son, that whosoever believeth in him should not perish, but have everlasting life." John 3:16 (KJV). When God said he loved us, he also demonstrated that love by sending his Son to take our place on the cross. He put love into action. There are many people saying that they love you, but their definition of love is dependent on "if they do something for you, you have to do something for them in return!" I believe true love is when we can reach out to people and minister to them in whatever way we can with no strings attached, just as GOD did. ***"But God commendeth his love toward us, in that, while we were yet sinners, Christ died for us."* Romans 5:8 (KJV).**

I grew up in a neighbourhood where the community raised the children. By this I mean that parents looked out for other parents' children, which included correction as well. Every mother and father was everybody's mother and father in the neighbourhood. I felt the warmth and comfort of the other parents. If I was doing something wrong, I knew they had the privilege of correcting all the children in the neighbourhood, so for me there was no escaping it. When we knew other parents were looking out for us we couldn't do anything we wanted to, even though our parents were not at home.

I will share with you one memory. As a boy, I would often go by the river without consent, steal mangoes, oranges, coconuts, and so on. I loved hunting, so at times I left my home without consent while my parents were out and tried to be back before they returned. Sometimes I made it, and other times I failed miserably! You can just guess what my reward was; a good spanking was my due either way because in the absence of my parents, I had other eyes on me. So, whether my parents physically caught me in the act or not, the truth is, they always caught me. Nevertheless, as soon as I got the opportunity, I was gone again.

My parents did their best to bring us up in the best way they could by giving us the basic necessities. There were some days when things were very difficult. Mom was a dedicated housewife and dad was employed at a supermarket. He laboured there to take care of his family. There were times my parents did not have the cash to do what they wanted to, but they always taught us to be content with what we had. The slogan was, "If we have fig and salt to eat, the neighbour does not have to know." We kept that slogan throughout our family, and it still works for us today.

I remember there was a period where we had to survive on "top and bottom" for a few weeks. By this I mean we had to eat dasheen and dasheen leaves as a meal. Sometimes my parents would change to "choir girls," that is, smoke herrings. What we had, we made it sufficient, and our parents did their best to make us comfortable. *Parents don't try to give your children everything they ask for to make them feel you always have. Let them know that life has the up days and the down days. Let them know that some days would be rough while others would be smooth.* I remember there was one time we borrowed money to send my wife on a short vacation. Subsequently, I overheard my son on the phone requesting two pairs of brand name sneakers, so I asked him if he thought we were "big shots," to which his answer was, "Yes!" We didn't tell him we had to borrow the money for the vacation. That day, I learned my lesson and I began to let my children know some of the stuff we go through as a family. Before that experience, when our children asked for things, if we did not have the money, we borrowed to make sure they got what they wanted. We then recognized that we did not need to play who we were not. We needed to make them aware that we live in a real-world and are faced with real challenges like everyone else.

When we are faced with challenges and go through them, we can train our children to face their challenges and come out victorious. To me, experience is one of the greatest teachers of all time. We need to raise this generation right, otherwise, we will produce one worse than ours. We need to teach our children to trust GOD. If parents don't know how to, and never learned themselves to trust God, how then can they teach their children to trust Him? (Proverbs 3:5-6) We need to teach them to walk by faith. But if as parents, we never learned to walk by faith, it would be impossible to teach our kids to do so. Paul reminded Timothy in 2 Timothy 1:5 about the unmovable faith that was in him: faith that was first in his grandmother Lois and his mother Eunice. Paul recalled that this faith had filtered down to Timothy. Paul did not have to teach Timothy about faith as he was convinced he had that faith based on what he saw in Paul which stemmed from his grandmother and mother.

Children learn from their parents, that's why we need to teach them right and be good examples to them. For example, as parents, I believe, if we don't want our children to smoke, even if we do, we must not smoke in front of them or we should give up the habit completely. Some parents even ask their children to light the cigarette while some ask their kids to purchase them, and when their children begin to smoke, they resort to scolding them. I can never recall my father or mother to be drinkers or smokers. I can say they are splendid examples to us. As I write, both are still alive and happily married for over forty years.

I know my father to be a man who loves to read the book of Psalms and pray. I have never heard my father and mother have a misunderstanding or accusing one another of being unfaithful. I never saw them not speaking to each other for days, nor have I heard them using obscene language to each other or swearing what they would do to each other when the opportunity arises. I never heard them threatening one another with violence or even with a weapon. I'm not saying that they were saints. They had misunderstandings and still do, but there was a way they handled it between themselves that kept them loving each other. My mom is the type of person who would not worry over anything but take it to the Lord in prayer as the songwriter says, "We go through the pain all because we do not carry everything to God in prayer." We can trust Him to work it out for us. I remember someone asked me once if I beat or physically abused my wife, and my answer was, *I have never seen my father do so to my mother and so I don't.* **For I know him, that he will command his children and his household after him, and they shall keep the way of the LORD, to do justice and judgment; that the LORD may bring upon Abraham that which he hath spoken of him. Genesis 18:19 (KJV).**

The bible also says, Don't be a striker, Titus 1:7 (KJV). In Genesis 18:19, God had confidence in Abraham that he would command not just his children but his entire household. God knew Abraham "inside out," God knew that what He deposited in Abraham was enough for him to take diligent care of his family.

I want to encourage all men to be responsible as fathers. Fatherhood is a serious responsibility. To be there for your family, you need to first know God. Don't just say you know Him, but submit your life to Him and allow Him to be in control of your entire life. Fathers who have children and are failing to properly care for them need to get up from where you are, call or write, but somehow get in contact with your children now. Begin to take care of them. That's your responsibility. I mean, provide for them and be there for them. That is more than dropping off cash, grocery, or clothing. Do your part! I understand that maybe your dad was not there for you, but don't allow your child or children to go through the same experience you went through. You can do better than that. The law should not have to force you to get involved in your child's life. *The bible says, "But if any provide not for his own, and especially for those of his own house, he hath denied the faith, and is worse than an infidel.* **1 Timothy 5:8 (KJV).**

One of the things I admire about my dad is the way he took care of his family. Things were not always the best, but he never ran away from his responsibility; my dad worked very hard to take care of his family. Your family is your responsibility! Not someone else's! The challenges are great for fathers, but with God's wisdom, knowledge, and understanding, we can be true fathers. We need to connect to the true vine, which is the Lord Jesus Christ. Reflecting on what I saw my dad and mom do, they provided for us in the best way they knew by working hard.

A word of caution to fathers, don't just work and pass the money to the wives and believe your responsibility is over. In addition to providing financially, we still have to take the time to train our children. Training is primarily the duty of fathers.

"Train up a child in the way he should go: and when he is old, he will not depart from it." **Proverbs 22:6 (KJV)**. This training is expected to come from the fathers, so it's not enough to just provide finance, it's much more than that. Be guided and directed by the Holy Spirit. You know, when I think about fathers my mind goes back to the Prodigal son's father. His son asked for what was rightfully his, what his father had saved up for him. I believe that this father didn't have to let his son go, but he did not stop him. He allowed him to go. It was the choice of the son but dad continued to look out for his son. He knew what he had deposited in him over the years and that someday this son who left in haste would return to the fold. Even though it may have hurt dad's heart, he still allowed him to go. Remember, dad took the time to train him and he did a very good job! The bible says in **Luke 15:17-18** *(KJV) "And when he came to himself, he said, how many hired servants of my father have bread enough and to spare, and I perish with hunger! I will arise and go to my father and will say unto him, Father, I have sinned against heaven, and before thee,"* The prodigal son's father continued to love and look for his son that one day he would come to himself and return first to his heavenly father and then to his earthly father as well. This he did.

The prodigal son's father was connected to his heavenly father. For fathers to be effective, we must first reconnect to God. I say re-connect because we were once connected but became disconnected because of what Adam did in the garden of Eden. Our heavenly father is encouraging and challenging us to come back to him. That's the only way as fathers, we can be the true father God desires us to be. So, fathers as you read, God is waiting on us to reconnect to him that we can be true fathers on the face of the earth and be a true representative of our heavenly father to our children.

In Search of Me

I was always more developed in size for my age compared to other kids. So when I was about thirteen years old I looked like eighteen. I remember at age fourteen, I took my first smoke of a cigarette after being encouraged by some friends. I was visiting their home around Christmas time. I could not go home with the cigarette scent in my mouth because I knew I would get a good spanking so I washed my mouth with some powdered soap, which gave me a terrible burning. However, I was more concerned about saving myself from being scolded by my parents.

I also remember starting to work at a very young age. I was attending St. Kevin's College at this time and my parents were unable to pay the school fee and I was chastised in school for not having the fee. I decided then, that my parents were trying too hard to provide the school fee and I was still being disciplined for something outside of my control. When I saw the sacrifice my parents were making to send me to school and there were still five other children to take care of, and my dad's salary was small, I decided to quit school and get a job to support myself and my parents. My first job was at a Supermarket around the Christmas season. Following this, I worked at F.W. Woolworth and it went well. I was loved and admired by everyone because of the way I carried myself. I think I need to pause and thank God for my parents, for the teaching and training they instilled in me. There were some basic things they instilled like saying good morning or evening to the people in the neighbourhood and on the streets. They taught their kids to acknowledge God and pray and how to exhibit proper mannerism when responding to our elders. When the person was a female, "Yes miss" or "No miss" was the appropriate response. For a male "Yes or no sir."

We learned that if there was conflict in the home, we needed to forgive each other. If our parents and one of the neighbours had a misunderstanding, we dared not treat that person with scant courtesy, else you risked getting a scolding.

I often heard my parents say, "What begins at home would end abroad," meaning, what is practiced at home, positive or negative, influences what is done outside of the home. Charity begins at home, meaning, love begins in the home. If we practice it at home, we will take it out of the home.

Those were some of the values my parents instilled in me. This took me a very long way in life and I strive to pass these values on to my children and even others I meet.

I must confess, after the cigarette, I encountered another experience with drugs, this time alcohol. I subsequently became hooked on it due to the peer pressure of some co-workers who were seasoned drinkers. However, after experiencing the negative effects that alcohol had on me, such as vomiting and falling down whenever I consumed it, I left the alcohol.

I experienced a very conflicted teenage life. One of much curiosity and finding myself.

All this time my parents and other persons kept speaking to me; beckoning me to make a change. I listened to everyone but took the advice I believed would work for me; I went to another level.

Along my journey, while engaging in unhealthy behaviour at that time, a bible class started next door to my home and the owner of the home, Mother Molly, invited me. I accepted the invitation and accompanied my family a few times.

During that time, I was still engaged in wrongful acts, even heavier than before. Later I was introduced to another bible class, this time at a different Church. This church became my shelter whenever I did wrong and felt guilty afterwards. The preacher in the bible study class was assertive and he would tell you just as it is. At times, his words would scare me off. However, my old habits persisted.

There was another gentleman who would come ever so often to bring a gospel track and witness to me. This angered me but he never gave up; he kept encouraging me to give my heart to the Lord. This brother was persistent; however, I wanted no part. This continued until one day I became so ill, I felt like death would be my portion. I immediately began to reflect on all that was being said to me by various preachers all the while, and that day I made a verbal commitment to give my heart to the Lord if He saved my life. The prayers worked. However, as soon as I recovered, I changed plans and continued living my old lifestyle.

I started losing a few pounds every day because of my lifestyle. I knew I was going the wrong way. It was like I wanted to stop living this way but did not know how to go about doing it. I continued to attend the bible classes and slowly began to understand what the Pastors were preaching.

As I understood the word of God, I realized that if I died I would go to hell and not heaven, so I began to pray at nights. All the while my parents and other persons kept admonishing me. I listened, answered, and then went back to living my old life. The Bible says, no man can come unless the spirit of God draws him.

My prayer was this:

"Father, I know I am not doing the right thing, I know right from wrong, I know if I die now I will be going to hell, but God, help me to do the right thing, give me the strength ... Lord save me, and don't allow me to die in this condition. Lord, I want to go to heaven."

Allow me to mention that my parents never gave up on me. They continued to talk, warn and caution me about my ways, and I just kept going my "merry" way. At that time, I knew if I died then, where I would be going. My conscience was now troubling me very much and I had to do something and do it quickly. One evening, I went to hang out in the next trace where I would usually go—sitting on the curb wall, relaxing. The weather that evening was overcast, and lightning was flashing. I was afraid. I saw God in the lightning that evening. I don't care what anyone says, but I saw God! I remember every time the lightning flashed after the first time, I saw Him.

I turned to the other side to evade Him but whichever side I turned to, He was in the lightning just looking at me.

I knew it before, but on that evening if I did not before believe, I had to believe there and then that there is truly a God. From that time onward I was a different person. I knew my time was close to attending bible study at the Pentecostal Church, so I left to prepare myself. This was the night of all nights. I saw the preacher that night and when I looked at him, my words questioned him and his ability to preach. *He can't preach anything*, was one of my assumptions. I cannot remember how he began to talk about this emptiness on the inside but I felt empty on the inside and I was putting my hands on almost anything to fill that void. That was my life at the time: I was searching, and when the altar call was made I was at the altar before God that night.

However, I did not submit my life to God. I said the sinner's prayer like so many people do today who tell themselves that's it, 'I am saved' and never move one step further. The following year, I was playing pan in San Fernando with a steel band. The year after that, I was playing mas for the Carnival celebrations in our country, and the following year I had planned to play Wild Indian Mas.

The year 1978 is a memorable year for me. I had begun eating meat again the previous year (1977) and in August of 1978 my mother told me that there was baptism in that same month, to which I replied, "Not this year, next year after I finish play my mas." But God had other plans! Someone was praying for me. Someone was interceding for me. On the public holiday, 31st August, there was a "fete" march Bald Head Vs Weed Smokers, starting time 9.00 am. I remember on the 30th of August 1978, I came home from work, had an argument with my father, slammed the door in his face, and left. Little did I know I would meet great difficulty on the outside. That night I was held by the police for doing wrong.

The news had reached my parents that I was held by the police. My parents had always told me that they would not be visiting me in any police station the day that I got myself into trouble. Now, here I was.

Ironically, the first persons I saw after my arrest were my parents, who were tirelessly championing my cause. Owing to shame, I did not come to the front. They continued striving for the balance of the night and throughout Independence Day to get my bail. My most horrible time inside there was the first night. There were nine of us inside a cell that should have only held four persons. We asked one officer for some water to drink, and he filled a big white enamel cup and every one of us had to drink from the same cup. Just as the cup was about to be passed on to me, another officer who claimed that the cup was his, came and snatched it, saying, "this cup is mine," and threw away the water in front of my face. In my heart I said, *LORD, this is what I have to go through inside here.* My throat was very dry at that time.

I must confess, however, that jail cell was the place for me at that time because I had taken the freedom I had outside for granted. I had the opportunity to make a wise choice to serve God but did not do so before. But in that cell for the twelve or more hours God allowed me to remain inside there, He had the opportunity of speaking to me and I had to listen to Him. I reflected on my life as a video and God was speaking to me, I had nowhere to run. Before, I was too busy to listen, but there I was in a place where I just had to listen to the voice of God. He spoke and I listened! When God delivered me from prison, I still did not abandon my old life. I got bail and had to appear in court on the first of September, which I did, and was charged fifty dollars or thirty days hard labour.

On the twenty-fifth of October 1978, I decided (after weighing all the options) that a changed life was the best way to go. A very important part of this transformation was the love that my father and mother showed me while I was in crisis. Only then did I appreciate how much my parents loved me. Today I can say like the songwriter, "I was sinking deep in sin," and I can even go further and say, I knew why also. It was due to my own stubbornness and disobedient behaviour. I was sinking, but God's love in my parents' heart stretched forth hands and helped me out from my hopeless situation. Thank God for Jesus. I can say thank God for Jesus and for the spirit of repentance that enabled me to give my life to God.

There were two other persons who were very instrumental in my life: Mother Molly and Teacher Drakes—both now deceased. I remember Mother Molly would always make sure I had money to attend youth group sessions and Wednesday night and Sunday services. If I lacked, she made sure I had by giving me of her own. That meant so much to me, and more times than I can count, her actions went a long way in getting me to and from church. In my heart I was settled upon just getting baptized and going back to my old life. I heard at that time that, "Baptism is requisite," so to me, if you got baptized that was all that was needed.

Teacher Drakes also did her part by looking out for me and encouraging new Christian converts who had just submitted or given their lives to the Lord. She emphasized that this was not dolly house but serious business and no time to play. The bible says, *"... **work out your own salvation with fear and trembling.**"* **Philippians 2:12 (KJV).** Today, some persons are giving their hearts to God and attending services once in two months and settling for a gospel programme on television on Sunday mornings. However, *"**not forsaking the assembling of ourselves together as the manner of some is; but exhorting one another: and so much the more, as ye see the day approaching.**"* **Heb. 10:25** is another encouragement from scripture, which leads us to understanding the importance of a genuine walk with Christ. So also is **Matt 18:20 (KJV),** *"For where two or three are gathered together in my name, there am I in the midst of them."* and **Psalms 27:4 (KJV):** *"One thing have I desired of the LORD, that will I seek after; that I may dwell in the house of the LORD all the days of my life, to behold the beauty of the LORD, and to enquire in his temple."*

What I'm saying is this: we make time to go to work, shop, visit friends, and do every other thing that we need to do. We do not miss a day from our jobs because of our fear of losing a day's pay. Even though folks are sick, they still attempt to go to work. Then, why not make the effort and find yourself in the house of the Lord. Just as you make sacrifices to go to other places, make the sacrifice to serve God faithfully. As you read, if you are lackadaisical in this area, please at once, "pull up your socks." One spiritual meal cannot sustain you for the week, it is impossible! You will fall apart and crumble. I mean, you may fall through the crack when the storm comes because you do not know what the Word of God says. You get to know the Word of God when you listen, read, and meditate upon it. The bible says, faith comes by hearing. Hearing what? Not foolishness, gossip, nor lies, but the Word of God.

The more your faith increases, the more you will be able to face the challenges that will come your way on a daily basis. The bible says, His mercies are new every morning, and this will come when we align ourselves with God by fellowshipping with Him regularly. Fellowshipping with Him entails praying, reading His Word, and building a relationship with Him. We build a relationship with a person when we spend quality time with that person. If we are going to have a good relationship with our God, we need to spend more and more time with Him. The word of God says, *"If ye abide in me, and my words abide in you, ye shall ask what ye will, and it shall be done unto you."* **John 15:7 (KJV).** That word "abide" means to "stay in" so as much as we stay in God, we will get to know Him better. Know Him for His traits, His character and know Him for what He can do. I love the Apostle Paul's statement in **Philippians 3:10 (KJV)**, *"That I may know him, and the power of his resurrection, and the fellowship of his sufferings, being made conformable unto his death;"* You see, it's one thing to know God but it's much better to know Him not just for healing a headache or receiving a five dollars or fifty dollars' miracle, but it's better to have an experience with Him. I believe that's when we could boast about knowing God. A lot of us claim we know God but when we are faced with challenges our actions show otherwise. Isaiah says, *"In the year that king Uzziah died I saw also the Lord sitting upon a throne, high and lifted, and his train filled the temple."* **Isaiah 6:1 (KJV).** You see, God was always there, but Isaiah only saw Him when King Uzziah died! It seems here like Uzziah was obstructing Isaiah's view, so he was not seeing God even though He was there. Similarly, for many of us, God is here but we allow all sorts of things to take the place of God. So, while He is always seeing us, we are not always seeing Him. At times God has to move the clouds of money, jobs, loved ones, the car, the friends, husband, wife, girlfriend, boyfriend, and even children to grasp our attention. The bible says, *"It is he that sitteth upon the circle of the earth, and the inhabitants thereof are as grasshoppers; that stretcheth out the heavens as a curtain, and spreadeth them out as a tent to dwell in:"* **Isaiah 40:22 (KJV).**

Changed Life

After submitting my life to God and getting baptized on the twenty-fifth of October in 1978, life had just begun for me. Only then I understood the meaning of Matthew 6:33 (KJV) which says, "But seek ye first the kingdom of God, and his righteousness; and all these things shall be added unto you." I wanted to achieve everything in life, but I only began to enjoy life when I decided to seek God first. It was like a dream come true. *I want to take this opportunity to encourage you as you read this; if you know Him, get to know Him better, if you are in a backslidden state, return to Him right now and if you don't know Him at all, give your life to Him! It is the best decision you would ever make in your life. Maybe you have been contemplating this decision for a long time and have not yet made that commitment. You would never regret it: it's the most important decision you will ever make.*

As I write today, the eighteenth of November 2009, a gentleman came to me and said that he is fed-up with life. He said he's tried everything, and everything has failed him, and he wants to know what to do. I challenged him right there and then to give his life to the Lord, and I was willing to lead him to the Lord, to which he replied, "we would talk." Man was born with an inner vacuum, it's like a vacant space on the inside of both men and women. That space is to be filled by God Himself and while men and women are thirsty and desperate, looking for satisfaction in all the wrong places. Man must come to the place where he recognizes that God and God alone can fill that emptiness on the inside. I recognized it thirty years ago.

Following my baptism, I attended Mt. Beulah Spiritual Baptist Church. As I mentioned earlier, my intention was just to get baptized, but I was encouraged by a sister in the church to attend the youth group sessions, which I did. I was also encouraged by the other youths I saw at that time and I continued to attend. The youth group was fun. The president of the youth group took the time to teach us the Word of God. He used to take a Psalm and have everyone give a thought on a verse. It was scary at times but exciting at other times. The members of the youth group made it exciting. The youth group was special for us youths. The young men looked out for the young ladies, and if one person did not have money, that person was not left behind, we lived like a family. We went out a lot and interacted with other youths and that strengthened us and kept us together.

Attending youth group was exciting and so was bible study on Wednesday nights. Youths in our day attended Bible study. The youths were the ones who would visit the sick, minister, and pray for them and encourage them. We were also engaged in prayer meetings and choir practice! Thank God for a very charismatic and inspirational Pastor.

From then on, I grew in God. I learned to pray, read my bible, and build a relationship with God. I grew from strength to strength and was in fellowship as often as possible. I also attended every service. If you are reading this right now and you are a new believer or you desire to grow in God, I encourage you to attend all services in your local church, read your bible, and pray daily. Praying and meditating regularly upon God's Word are the foundational things we do to grow in God. The bible says, **"But grow in grace, and in the knowledge of our Lord and Saviour Jesus Christ. To him be glory both now and forever. Amen." 2 Peter 3:18 (KJV).** In order for a plant to grow it must get the necessary food. We must feed our spirits with the nutrients that would cause us to grow in Him. I wanted to grow, and I had a Pastor who pushed the youths to be the best they could be. He started a preachers' class; teaching the young men and women how to expound the word of God. Our church began producing vibrant young prayer warriors, preachers, and singers. The youth group multiplied as youths reached other youths. Young people were taught and released to preach, sing, pray, and excel in the other ministries. I excelled in prayer. I learned to pray, and occupied myself in other ministries like ushering and whatever I was asked to do. I served to the best of my ability and in God, I began to grow and mature.

God blessed me. I remained humble before Him; I don't like show business, I like pleasant things and people but not publicity because I believe that things of God are not show business. As the songwriter says, "All the glory must go to the Lord." I was asked to clean the church practically every day. I cleaned the washrooms because my Pastor liked the thorough job I did. I did so especially in preparation for service days which were on Sundays and Wednesdays and any other special services, and I did it with joy.

In doing so, I faced some challenges just like any other. There was one sister who always wanted to have her own way, she never wanted to sit in the pews. There were chairs reserved for use when the pews were filled and her preference, however, was to use the reserved chairs even though the ushers would advise her they were only to be used when the pews were filled. But with God's help and grace we the ushers coped with it.

At that time, I accompanied preachers from church to church and even carried the alias, "The Singing Evangelist." I took what I was doing very seriously. I would get my song, and play it over and over to learn it well. When I knew that I had an appointment, night after night I would spend time rehearsing; making sure I got it right. I also spent time in prayer as I learned the words of the song because it was not just opening my mouth and letting out air. I saw this as important as sharing the word of God. The result is God used me in a tremendous way in every church and crusade He took me to. The bible says, **"Whatsoever thy hand findeth to do, do it with thy might; for there is no work, nor device, nor knowledge, nor wisdom, in the grave, whither thou goest." Ecclesiastes 9:10 (KJV).**

Growing in God is very important. God called us not just to make up numbers and "warm the pews" or chairs. God called us to make other disciples. The bible says, we didn't choose God, but he chose us to be His witnesses. ***"Ye are my witnesses, saith the LORD, and my servant whom I have chosen: that ye may know and believe me, and understand that I am he: before me, there was no God formed, neither shall there be after me." *Isaiah 43:10 (KJV)**. One of the ways we can make disciples is by loving one another. I remember very early in my walk with God a brother offended me, and I was about to leave the church. When I took up the word of God to read that morning and opened the scriptures to the book of Ephesians, I cannot remember the exact scripture now. However, as I read that morning, God spoke to me through His word and that caused me to change my mind from walking out from not only the church, the brethren, and the Pastor, but also from walking out on God. You see, I know now, that plan was designed by the devil to take me out, but thank God for His mercy, grace, and wisdom.

My first thought on the offense, was how a young man who claimed to be a brother could do what he did? **I have grown to learn that the Devil, the thief, cometh not but for to steal, to kill, and to destroy but GOD hath come that you and I might have life and that we might have it more abundantly, found in John 10:10 (KJV)**. I want you to know, that the first three months of your walk with God are the most critical. This period of your walk with God is like when you enter a new job. You are on probation and everyone's eyes are on you. So, make up your mind to perform to the best of your ability. That is the time you must be punctual, be regular, and carry yourself properly. All the darts would be thrown at you for the first three months. Some make it and others don't. During probation, there are some, who despite what you do, you cannot please. Some fall by the wayside but after the three challenging months some also come out on top, not due to their physical strength or their will power, but their sole reliance on God.

The first three months, the devil would throw every dart at you, and it is not designed to build you, but to destroy you. You must make up your mind, be determined to be strong, to persevere, and despite what happens, you do not give up or give in. You have to make up your mind to refuse to give up, refuse to give in knowing that the word of God says, ***"I can do all things through Christ which strengtheneth me,"* Philippians 4:13 (KJV).** So, with God's help and strength you can pass your probationary period on your secular job and also your probation in God with "flying colours" because you did not depend upon your strength and wisdom but you depended upon God and God alone. As such, you would not just be successful for three months but will be successful throughout all the years that God would choose to have you on the face of the earth. You need to be dependent on God as the songwriter says, "Trust him where you cannot trace Him."

Meeting My Bride

I continued to grow in God and walked faithfully before Him and began to excel in the things of God. With the encouragement of the young brethren and prayerful support, I continued to serve God. After about two years, I blessed my eyes on a charming young lady and there was a connection between us, even though I never told her anything. We only looked at each other and smiled. One of the things I thank God for is this: after about two years of being saved, I moved into my Pastor's home and had the encouragement of him and his wonderful family looking out for me. It was challenging, but God used that time to mould and shape my life into a fine respectable young man, living for God and loving Him. They looked out for me, and I thank God for that period. While that was going on though, the young people who I met in youth group were dating, moving on, and getting married. The charming young lady, who today is my wife, and I, were attending those weddings as bridesmaid and groomsman. I took her to all weddings until our turn came!

We had attended at least five weddings together before we took that giant step on August 6, 1983. Her dad died about a year after we met, but while he was alive, I could not visit her at home. Furthermore, my Pastor never allowed that. When he found out that I had seen a young lady I liked, and it was confirmed, he immediately sent me home to inform my parents, which I did. It was only then he allowed an elder to accompany me to the young sister's home to inform her parents. He did not want anything going on between the young people that he was not aware of. The church was then informed that Wayne liked Ann. He watched me like a hawk! We could not hold hands nor kiss! As youths, we were always informed not to go to places where there was no one around. He said plainly, "You would do funny things." He always said, any time two people who like each other go to places and nobody is around, you would do funny things. It's a fact, so he was stern.

I want to encourage the young couples who are reading this book, if you like each other, take this advice. It is advisable to go out in groups. You could get into trouble for a lack of self-control. ***Abstain from all appearance of evil.* 1 Thessalonians. 5:22 (KJV)**. I did not get myself into trouble because I did not get the opportunity. But who knows if it was today; times are different. Many women seem to be more aggressive than the men, even Christian women. I remember seeing a sister one night in her veranda in the dark with a young man. I didn't see them doing anything unscriptural, but I still called her another day and cautioned her. She replied, "Pastor, you don't know I have control?" and laughed it off. A few months later I observed her face getting fat like when you blow up a balloon and said, *"Sister you have control."* Now her response was, "Pastor, I thought I had control, but I didn't."

I reminded her of my advice to her. The result was a baby nine months later, all because she found herself with a young man whom she had a liking for, in the wrong place and at the wrong time. So new generation of Christians please take heed.

When people feel attracted to each other, you choose to play with one another's hand, it's simple. Then, you would want to move from the hands to somewhere else on the body. If you begin kissing, especially passionate kissing, or want to play with each other's face, sooner or later you would get yourself into trouble that you can't handle. So, establish guidelines and boundaries that will help you wait until you walk down the aisle with the young man or woman. You need to know when 'the honey comes out of the moon, there would not be any more honeymoon!' The honeymoon is only for those who would wait. Leave the honey on the moon until the wedding night, that's the only time when you can have a honeymoon.

One might ask, how can you leave the honey in the moon? Young people, when you depend upon the Holy Spirit who can keep you and bring that sexual desire under control until you are married. Jesus said, if he didn't go the Comforter would not come, and that's part of the job of the Holy Spirit in our lives, to bring all our uncontrolled desires under total control. ***Nevertheless, I tell you the truth; It is expedient for you that I go away: for if I go not away, the Comforter will not come unto you; but if I depart, I will send him unto you,* John 16:7 (KJV)**. I am not talking just from hearsay but from experience. I have experienced the Holy Spirit's controlling power time and time again in my life. The bible says the unruliest member in our body is the tongue. If we would allow the Holy Spirit to bring that area of our lives under control He would, but we must allow Him to, just as we would for any other area of our lives.

I continued to live for God and tried my best to attend all services, even though I was working a shift system. When rostered to work, I worked, but when I was off, I was in church, and I am talking about coming from a ten to six shift on a Sunday morning. It was and is still a sacrifice because as I write I still work shift and make myself available in church as regularly as possible. A word of encouragement to Christians who work shift, *it may not be easy*. I know of many Christians who work shift and do not make the sacrifice to attend service. I choose, however, that even if I work all night, half night, or a quarter of the night, when it is Sunday morning, I get an extra strength and I am so excited to attend service that I cannot stay home to rest. I have seen God bless me through making this sacrifice throughout the years and some of the same persons who go home and claim they are going to sleep on a Sunday morning, find themselves not sleeping but doing work at home.

When we make sacrifices for God, He will go the extra mile for us. The same Christian brother or sister who would claim they are too tired to attend service, when it's time for work find all the strength in the world to do so. Why? Because at the end of the week, fortnight or month, they don't want their salaries to be short. These same individuals would not make the sacrifice for God. At times when we see other brethren blessed who chose to make the sacrifice, we envy them. We know that mere church attendance doesn't save anyone. There are a lot of people hiding under the church banner. We could be in church and "Split hell wide open" if we don't have a relationship with God and choose to live for Him faithfully. The church is our meeting place of fellowship where we go and refuel to continue doing the will of God. There are three basic things I look at, that I believe a person who decides to follow God faithfully must do: (1) Read the bible. (2) Learn to pray and be a good intercessor. (3) Make time to fellowship. There is much more that we need to do but we must start somewhere, and this is a good place to start.

I thank God that I learned to pray and had a great love for God and still do. After getting married in 1983, I was excited. Before I go any further, I must say this—while dating my wife (who came from a single-parent home), there were some senior people in the church whom I met serving God. At that time, they were called mothers and teachers in the faith. Some pulled me aside and openly told me don't marry my present wife because her mother was a single parent who had faced some challenges bringing them up. I listened to those senior ones and told them okay. I, however, wondered about this advice. There is a saying, "If you have glass windows don't pelt stones." Some of those mothers and teachers had daughters and there was a section of the seniors at that time who tried to play matchmakers. I thank God that even though I was considered a "young giddy head Christian" as I heard one Mother refer to me, that I depended upon God for everything, and He saw me through when I found my bride and we got married.

We did not have any form of counselling as this generation has today. We got married based on pure love. We faced some challenges after two years of our marriage just like other married couples, but I thank God that I knew how to pray. I bought and read good books, prayed a lot, sought God, and He helped us. I thank God today for this generation who have some of the best counsellors, good literature, and in some cases good examples. Yet still, some couples don't decide to buckle down and enjoy their lives. *I encourage young, middle age and senior married couples today: you may be facing some of the greatest challenges of your life in marriage, but trust God and hold on to your marriage. Men fight for your marriage! Pray, fast, and seek God's face. Take whatever counselling you can get, but purpose in your heart to remain married. Remember, marriage is not for until you experience problems or obstacles; rather, marriage is for a lifetime—until death do you and your wife part.* **For this cause shall a man leave his father and mother, and shall be joined unto his wife, and they two shall be one flesh. Ephesians 5:31 (KJV).**

As Christians, we need to know God. If I did not have a relationship with Him, I would have been moved by those senior members' wrong counsel. When you enter a church, you can experience all kinds of obstacles along the way. However, these are things that happen to us growing up, whether as a Christian or not and we are being prepared for such a time like this. If we can look back and reflect, we would realize that some of the things God allowed us to go through, God did not allow it to kill us, but He preserved our lives just as He did with Joseph. He is getting us ready for a life down the road. *So, brother, sister, you may be facing the greatest test of your life, you need to remember, you would not have a testimony without a test. You must be tested!* We can only overcome the devil according to **Rev 12:11 (KJV)** which says, ***And they overcame him by the blood of the Lamb, and by the word of their testimony, and they loved not their lives unto the death.*** Remember, God did not save us to serve the Pastor, a brother, or sister, God saved us to serve Him. As such, even though somebody in the fellowship does us wrong, God did not do us anything. We are called to serve God and not man. Stay focused and serve God faithfully. ***Yea, and all that will live godly in Christ Jesus shall suffer persecution.* II Timothy 3:12 (KJV).** I faced my challenges with God at my side or God at the head, and I'm still facing challenges and the God of Israel is still seeing me, my family, and the brethren through.

A word of caution to husbands and wives. Don't listen to gossip about your spouse. I went through that period and was listening to gossip about my wife and my marriage and was most miserable. At that time there was always quarrelling, accusing, and pointing fingers in my home. I thank God for the Holy Spirit who spoke to me and told me very distinctly, to stop listening to people. I was obedient and the conflicts, pointing fingers, and accusations stopped immediately, so take heed.

I remember in my Christian walk, I kept trusting God, allowing Him to oversee my life. After eleven years of continuous work, I got laid off from my job at the Iron and Steel Company of Trinidad and Tobago (ISCOTT). I was a bit worried. About three months later, my wife lost her job. At that time, we already had our first child Dwayne a.k.a. Silent Sah. To be honest, I complained, I questioned God, I wanted answers as to why this had happened to us. It was said at that time, there was a recession. We tried to migrate, but I have to say, God did not allow it. I cried, but God was processing us, and we did not know. God took us from living off thousands to living off a few hundred dollars, but we ate, drank, and lived a comfortable life. During that time out of a job, God opened a door for me to attend Bible School, which I always had a desire to attend. What kept me at this time was the Word of God, ***Though he slay me, yet will I trust in him: but I will maintain mine own ways before him.*** **Job 13:15 (KJV).** When I was about to graduate from Bible School, God re-opened the job door for me.

I got a better job opportunity than the one I had before and could at least get a proper rest at night. God always has something better in store for us, but we are sometimes afraid of processing; we only want to experience the blessings of God, but good things don't come easy. We must make up our minds to work for it. God took us through and after two years, I was on a new job. What I told people and still hold fast to, is this: the money that I would have made in that two years could not compare to the relationship I now have with God. God wants us to be solely dependent upon Him and not rely on anyone else. When I got laid off from my previous job, I was a faithful tithe payer, I gave gifts, paid pledges, and walked faithfully before God. I also thought that good things used to happen to good people and terrible things happened to bad people. But God is no respecter of persons. He allows the rain to fall on the just and the unjust. He is not biased; He doesn't take sides. If God sees we need processing, He is going to process us whether we like it or not. Whether we sanction it or not, we are going to be processed.

We had our second child within one year and that was very challenging. We now had two babies in two years, but God made it easy for us by blessing us with another boy so, our first son's clothes were used for the second. God always has a plan that you and I don't know about. Within this time, we experienced a church split. It was not easy to handle the split but even in that challenging time, God kept us and preserved our spiritual lives. Some members chose to leave, some stayed and some of the brethren got an opportunity to do what they've always wanted to do or what they had locked up in their hearts a long time ago. When the space was too 'hot' in our church, we attended another church just to keep in fellowship with God. When things 'cooled' down we were back there again, until God calmed the storm that was blowing so hard at that time. Every storm will come to a calm and that storm came to a calm. At times God allows the storms to blow in our lives and against us, but it's not directed to destroy us but to make our lives much better than before. When we thought we were unable to make it, God had already provided a way out for us. I say to you, *'no matter how tough it looks or appears, God has already made a way out, so keep focus. Keep your eyes upon the Lord and look Him straight in His wonderful face.'*

I remember having to take care of two babies and questioning God. At the same time, I had to handle Bible School, not knowing that God was preparing me to become the Pastor of the church where I was the then assistant Pastor. God prepared me with my two children. He was getting me ready to lead from the front, but I didn't know. It was not long after, the Pastor of the Church was moving to begin a church plant in another community and the work was handed over to me. Thank God for the training at Bible School and with my own children—it prepared me for the task that God had ahead for me and which I knew nothing about. I took up the mantle and moved forward. At times it was not easy, but God saw my wife and I through as we walked in obedience to His call upon our lives.

It was very exciting, very nice, and at times I wondered what I was doing with that shoe on. But I am here simply because I believe in my heart that not just I, but we are called by Almighty God for such a time like this. If God did not call us or I did not believe God called me, I would have walked away already, but I am still here because of the call of God on my life.

I remember our church having an attendance between thirty-five to forty persons on Sundays. We experienced different things happening from time to time just as I took over the leadership of the church. We hosted a Bar-B-Que and after that event, it was like we had opened the door for the enemy to come in. There was increasing confusion which I had to address. I remember when the first person left the church, I had to take counselling. Ten years later when someone left, I lifted my hands and praised God. We Pastors, at times must lift our hands and say thank you Lord, when these things happen.

The confusion that broke out showed up our immaturity to host functions at that time. There were some minor issues that the enemy used to cause confusion among the brethren. I thank God for the prayer warriors, intercessors, and the wisdom and knowledge of God, that put the devil in his rightful place. There must be prayer warriors and intercessors in every local church.

I attended Bible School for two years (1988-1990) and I was named the preacher of the class. Bible School did not make me a preacher, an evangelist, apostle nor a prophet; it was a contributing factor.

A word of caution to the wise! Some people attend Bible School and then want to take over the church. They discover that their Pastor does not know anything and so they want to stage a coup in the church. Remember Korah and the others who opposed Moses in the wilderness and how God dealt with them. Don't let this be you.

It is exciting to attend Bible School but don't get beside yourself to feel you have arrived, knowing more than your Pastor. Mr., Mrs., Sis, Bro, lady and gentleman, don't lose respect for God's servant. You might have more knowledge than your Pastor and his wife in some areas, but do not lose respect. Please don't try to fight your Pastor. God has a way of doing things that in simple words we don't understand. Allow him to work it out. Instead of finding all the faults about your Pastor, choose to pray for him/her and spouse. Trust that God will change your Pastor.

I heard of this staff who had a problem with their Pastor, and you know what they chose to do? They arrived for work one hour earlier every day. I think even the Pastor questioned their early arrival. Guess what, they were coming in early every day to use that hour to pray for their Pastor that God will bring change to his life. The God of miracles, might, and power came through for that staff. It was like when the church was praying for Peter, and God delivered him miraculously while they were praying. God came through, changed him, changed his ways, changed his attitude, changed his mind-set, and placed him back on the right track.

When the church in the book of Acts (chapter 12) prayed in unity, agreement, and one accord, there were several things that God did. As the church prayed, yokes were broken, and literal chains fell off Peter. An angel was dispatched to that prison and as the church continued to pray, God opened the iron gates, woke up Peter, leading him in the right direction. Prayer caused the angel to lead Peter in the right direction. If the church continues to pray in unity and sincerity, we will experience God's awesome power. God has so much He wants to do for the church, but we must walk in obedience to His word. When Paul and Silas were in prison what did they do? They praised and prayed to the God of Israel and at midnight God came through for them. It was not just prayer, but it was united prayer and praise, mixed with faith, they believed God and God came through for them. I'd say or put it this way: the church can allow and block things from happening. The church was sitting down because they allowed James to be killed and Peter was going to be killed also, but the Church realised if they didn't do something then, they might be sorry. So, pray until something happens! Pray until there is a complete turnaround of the situation! The bible says when the church prays God could change the hearts of men and women who are considered hard and are refusing to change. Even our loved ones and children, God is able to change through prayer.

Four months after our first son was born, in December of 1984, I experienced God's shifting to change my circumstances through the power of prayer. My job at the time was a security officer. Part of my job and another officer's was to secure the company vehicles at nights and the keys were left in our care. However, the officers use to take their chance and drive the company vehicles. My father always told his children don't follow a multitude to do evil in reference to **Exodus 23:2 (KJV)**. At that time, I was going for my license and thought it fit, upon seeing the other guys driving and getting away with it, to take some practice on the company vehicle. I did this the first evening shift and it felt very good. I came home and told my mom who said to me, "Wayne leave the people vehicle alone." I heard her but did not take heed, and on my next evening shift, I took the company vehicle and drove it again. I did everything right but while going to park the vehicle I ran the vehicle into a drain right in front of my co-worker who didn't know the Lord. When I came out and saw the damage to the vehicle, my actual words were, *Wayne, you just lost your job.* My Corporal had already left for home. I left the compound that Friday night without reporting the accident and came home very much afraid. In those days they had what was called Movie Night, so I decided to watch some movies that night. But I could not understand what was going on because of the fear that someone would report me. I remember waking my wife and telling her what had happened and also for a little comfort, she only raised her head and said, "eh heh, eh heh," not knowing how scared I was at that time.

The next day, which was Saturday morning, for every dog I heard barking, I was looking up the hill to see if someone from my job was coming. I remember going to church on Sunday morning and at church, I don't know if I appeared to be worried, but my sister, Charmene, came to me and asked, "Bedeau what happen?" I opened up and told her what had happened. She asked, "What did you do?" *I told her that I did not report it* and she replied, "You know what to do when you go back to work, go and report it, and tell your seniors what took place." I answered her very politely and after the conversation, I thought, *"she mad that is loss work."* That same morning, I was asked to carry on the prayer meeting. I was discouraged, I needed encouragement but had to encourage others. I pushed through it. I went back to work the Sunday night and by then my corporal had found out about the accident, and he agreed that he would take the 'rap' for me, declaring that it was him who was driving the vehicle. However, my conscience worried me. My co-worker at the time of the accident said, if he was asked, he would say it was me and right at that moment, the Lord gave me the strength and I told my corporal I will go to the Chief Security Officer and confess to damaging the vehicle. My corporal and all my other co-workers were in shock at my confession of the matter.

If I concealed or covered up the truth it would have blown back up in my face sometime down the road and my workers would always have something against me; I did not want that. My corporal arranged for me to meet with the Chief Security Officer and the Monday morning at nine, I walked into his office without hesitation. The minute we exchanged greetings, he said, "Have a seat," which I did. His next question was, "What can I do for you?" Right away I said, *Sir, the vehicle that's damaged, I am the person who was driving.* The man was in shock. They had already formed in their mind an idea of who was responsible for the incident and it was not me. His next question was, "How that happened to you, you are a Christian?" My reply was, *Sir, I am going to get my license and I was taking a little practice.* He looked at me and said, "I cannot help you, I helped other people already, but I can't help you." I did not speak loudly but I said, *God you can.*

He further told me, the Sergeant will take a statement from me, which he did, and I will hear from them. He also told me that this license would cost me a bit and after about a month I was called in again. This time I was told how much I needed to pay for the damage. My weekly salary was three hundred and fifty dollars, and after tax, health surcharge, and national insurance deductions, it was just a little over two hundred dollars, I can't remember the exact amount. The manager, Mr. Winston Andrews, now deceased, told me to go home, discuss it with my wife and come back and tell him how much I can pay a week. I had to pay the excess for the vehicle's insurance which was fifteen hundred dollars. We decided that we would pay fifty dollars per week which went on for thirty weeks, and we survived.

While making the payments, I could only afford twenty dollars in the Credit Union. On completion I decided, if we could survive for thirty weeks while making the payment, we could continue without these fifty dollars. I then diverted the fifty dollars to add to the twenty dollars Credit Union saving, and instead of just saving twenty I was saving seventy dollars.

The bible says, and I paraphrase, **what is meant for evil God has the ability to turn around and bring good out of it. Genesis 50:20.** I must also confess, God has a way of "pulling up our socks" and waking us up when we start to nod on ourselves.

I had a blue bible in my cupboard at my workplace that I usually read every day because I had the time when things cooled down on evenings. For some reason or the other, the bible could not come out of the cupboard anymore and all the jokes my co-workers made I would be laughing at and listening to all the filthy conversations. From the minute the car reached into the drain I saw the blue bible in front of me. Nobody brought it, but it appeared, I wanted to read it right there and then. Truth be told, since that accident, from the next tour of duty, no one had to tell me to take it and read it, I knew I had to read my bible. I thank God for giving me a wakeup call, it could have been worse. What I saw was God's hand of love towards me, His kindness, His faithfulness, and even His greatness and also His discipline towards me and my family. Had I lost my job at that time, it would not have been the Devil nor anyone to blame, but my disobedience. Thank God for His mercy and grace towards me. This encouraged me and my family to continue serving God because we knew that God loved us with an everlasting love. The bible says, who God loves he chastens, "*For whom the Lord loveth he chasteneth, and scourgeth every son whom he receiveth. Now no chastening for the present seemeth to be joyous, but grievous: nevertheless, afterward, it yieldeth the peaceable fruit of righteousness unto them which are exercised thereby.* **Hebrews. 12:6, 11 (KJV).**"

Just as the word of God says, the chastening was not so nice because I was embarrassed that my co-workers knew and they in turn embarrassed me.

Thank God for His strength, courage, and boldness. The bible says, *"For a just man falleth seven times, and riseth up again: but the wicked shall fall into mischief."* **Proverbs 24:16 (KJV).** The problem is not in falling, no one likes to fall; not even a baby. A lot of people fall daily all around the world. Some have chosen to get up while some are still lying on the ground. Whosoever is reading this right now, mom, dad, aunty, uncle, brother, sister, grandad, grandma, cousin, mother-in-Law, father-in-Law, step-son, step-daughter, outcast, those who people have given up on, those who have been rejected by your closest relative, or maybe you are incarcerated, this is a prophetic word to you. *I say get up, arise in the name of Jesus Christ of Nazareth, get up from where you are sitting or lying, get up in Jesus' Name.* Some of you are not even trying to get up, maybe you have given up on life, on your future, on your vision, or on your dream, remember what God says about you and what will happen to you and your family. Wake up from your drowsy sleep, clean your eyes, go wash your face, and open your eyes once again.

Look at the man at the pool of Bethesda in John chapter five. People might wonder, given that there were so many people at the pool (all kinds of sick people with different types of diseases), Jesus went specifically to this man and told him to take up his bed and walk. If you read the account carefully, you would see that this man was trying, every time the angel came and troubled the water. He was trying to get into the pool to be healed, but he said, and I paraphrase, *every time I try somebody was getting in before me. He never gave up.* Jesus came to that man and in my opinion, what he was saying to him was, "you don't need to wait on another season to get into the pool. Your season is right now and here. I have been looking at you for the longest while and see that you desire to be healed." With all that being said, Jesus still asked him of his desire to be made whole. The man replied in the affirmative. Well then take up your bed and walk with it!

In developing the WD40 product, it is said that they tried it thirty-nine times and failed. On the fortieth attempt, it succeeded. Michael Jordan was dropped from his school's basketball team and resigned as the world's best basketball player. He is now inducted into the basketball hall of fame.

This is about the third time I am writing. The first time the papers were misplaced. The second time they were burnt. If I gave up due to all the obstacles I faced, I would not continue writing as I am doing. If you ask me where I am getting the money from to print and publish, I can't answer but I am writing, and it will be printed and published. God knows how; He is my provider and source. At present, I am working during the day and have decided if every night I write at least a page or a page and a half or even half of a page, I will finish it, but I need to do something.

When I started working at F. W. Woolworth, my salary was twenty-five dollars per week. From that, I saved, gave to my parents, and travelled. Then it began to increase, that was in 1974, and by 1982, I was taking home one hundred and seventy-five dollars per week. I had just met my girlfriend, now my wife, and after dating for about three years, we got married. That's when I knew I had to look for another job since one hundred and seventy-five dollars per week could not maintain my wife and me. My job hunt began, and I found a job at the Iron and Steel Company of Trinidad and Tobago. *Young man if you desire to get married, first thing first. Look for a job that can take care of both you and your wife. I know what faith is but, still, look for a job. Faith cannot take care of a wife.*

On the 2nd of December 1998, I was laid off from my job of nine years as a fireman at Caribbean Ispatt Ltd. I remember when I was sent home, my last son Joshua Jabari was just four months old. I wondered how I would take care of him, but God is the supplier of all our needs. He didn't make a mistake. Pastor David Lewis, my good friend and brother in the Lord, invited me to preach at his church the last Sunday before Christmas that same year and told me to bring my family. I hired a car and went to fulfil the engagement. When I walked into the church that morning, I observed the front of the altar filled with grocery items but did not know what was taking place. At the end of the service, Pastor David said, Pastor Bedeau this is for you and your family. The car we hired was a Royal Saloon which fortunately had a large trunk, so everything was able to fit. It was the first Christmas I had a full case of Peardrax in my home. We got everything we needed for the Christmas holidays; including drinks and groceries that lasted through December, January, and into the late part of February.

I remember one day opening the cupboard and realizing it was emptying, I said to myself, *Wayne you need to look for a job.* My friend, God, is no respecter of person. I got a job but did not go out and look nor even lift one finger. God allowed an insurance agent to call my home to set up an appointment with me, but instead, I told him the position I was in at the time did not allow me to buy insurance. The agent then offered me a job, which I did not refuse. The job entailed being a Financial Advisor Insurance Agent. I had never sold insurance before, but I believed whatsoever I put my hands to do, I would succeed and this I did. I sold insurance for at least one year, with success, until I decided to go to America which I did for five months.

My wife and I were facing some challenges in our marriage. At that time, we had our two sons, Dwayne and Swayne, and wanted a girl child. This was in 1989. We had tried before but without success. On new year's morning when we came from church, we talked, agreed, and then prayed. Nine months later the result was a beautiful baby girl who we named Rachel Annril Bedeau. The word of God says, *"Again I say unto you, That if two of you shall agree on earth as touching anything that they shall ask, it shall be done for them of my Father which is in heaven."* **Matt 18:19 (KJV).** When God blessed our family with that girl child there was a complete turnaround in my marriage. During those times I tried my best to stay faithful to God and He kept me and my family. Those were the years when my wife used to travel a lot due to some financial challenges we faced. We were also trying to accumulate money to build or buy a home, but the money was never enough. There were days I could not even send my children to school because I did not have the money, but God remained faithful. Around that time, as the church began to grow, I was faced with some serious issues in the church. I tell folks any time a church begins to grow financially, spiritually, and numerically, look out for attacks, and that is what was going on in the church at that time. I had to deal with some indiscipline, disobedience, and confusion with some of the brethren. It was like counselling and talking to, praying for, and coming against those strongholds in the lives of the brethren through prayer and fasting which caused those strongholds to be broken over the lives of the brethren. Then I decided to preach and teach on the topic of tithing. We immediately had results. Some of the brethren received the word and acted upon it but there was a small group who had problems with tithing and encouraged other brethren not to pay tithes. I stood my ground and continued to preach and teach the word of God and prayed. I saw the hand of God in a mighty way in our local church.

God is so amazing! Going through the toughest period in my life as a father, Pastor, and leader of my family, God has never left. When my wife and I got retrenched from our jobs we had difficulty paying the church rent because of our loss of income. I recalled one month we wrote a cheque for the rent and that cheque was returned for insufficient funds. As the leader, I was so embarrassed. Instead of passing in the front street, I started passing on the back street. But God be praised! We were believing God to provide the money but did not get it on time and the cheque was sent back to us.

I travelled to the United States in 1999 due to some serious financial difficulties. I did not have a place to stay but God provided a place at the right time. I left Trinidad with one twenty USD note and God gave me favour when I arrived in America. After facing some challenges, God used me to minister to all kinds of people, pray for them, counsel them and encourage them; letting them know that God would come through for them. While in United States, I can recall a woman called from the immigration office requesting prayer for an extension which she was not getting. When the Lord used me to pray, He came through for her right there and then. I experienced God in a unique way in America and He gave me favour with Ministers and opened doors for me to minister His word.

God allowed people to rough me up and toughen me up. He allowed people to hurt me and at one time I even got lost. But it was all in preparation for the task ahead: to return to Trinidad at the appointed time and deal with some issues in the local church which I did.

My last son Joshua Jabari Bedeau was born in 1997, 21st August. Around that time, it was tough in the church. While my wife was pregnant, the Lord led me to study the book of Joshua. Joshua means saves or Jehovah is salvation. I told my wife that we would name our son Joshua. We had not yet done an ultrasound, but I kept on declaring to her, *It's a boy! It's a boy!* Her blood pressure spiked most of the time and she had to be hospitalized on two occasions. However, I stood on the Word of God which declares, *I will never leave thee, nor forsake thee, also lo, I am with you always, even unto the end of the world.* When the child was born, he was a bouncing baby boy. He, like my daughter, brought joy to the family. Thank God for the prayers of the saints of God. Just as my daughter is, that child is a blessing to the family and to many other people who have encountered him. His other name is Jabari which means leader, and he is truly a leader and not a follower.

Some of the conflicts I was repeatedly dealing with were the spirits of division and confusion. I had to do a lot of talking, counselling, praying, and fasting. The conflict was between two families. It was only while in the USA, God gave me the grace, strength, and wisdom to deal with those spirits that were making havoc in our local church. With God's help, I dealt with it after returning from five months abroad. A short while after, both families left the local church. We saw a decrease in the confusion in our local church. God opened the door for me to go to the USA just to prepare me for the challenges that were ahead. Isn't He a loving God? **Genesis 50:20 (KJV)** *says, "But as for you, ye thought evil against me; but God meant it unto good, to bring to pass, as it is this day, to save much people alive."* I remember returning from the USA on March 2nd, 2001, and I began looking for a job but could not find any. I can recall saying to my wife, *I am going to look for coconut and make some coconut drops and pholourie.* I asked my mom to show me how to make the pholourie, which she did.

I did not have a health badge, but my family's wellbeing was at stake, so I started to sell pholourie and coconut drops while I applied for my health badge. The first day I went out, within a short period, the pholourie and drops were all sold out. We began to think and increased from pholourie and drops to fried nuts, currants roll, mango anchar, and kurma. I was now moving through the village selling these products. Where there is a will there is a way! We had four children at that time and they were all attending school. It was a bit challenging because we had to prepare the products in the day and after helping to make the things, I had to go out on the evenings to sell. I did not have a car, so I walked. I remember one day someone asked me, "Pastor Bedeau, how you are getting so small?" When I looked at myself I remembered that I was walking through the village every evening to sell. So, it was a twofold blessing. I was engaged in a family business to provide for my family and keeping fit at the same time.

I used to make at least ninety dollars per day during that period from the sales. Part of the proceeds were used to purchase items to prepare products for the next day; I was able to send my children to school and save.

December of that same year, 2001, I was able to give my wife money from the cash pan to make Christmas shopping. *Sometimes God wants to get the best out of us, but it only comes, at times, through the rough seasons.* Our business was doing well, customers telephoned to place orders during the day and I would deliver some in the evenings. I eventually got my health badge and after a few months, I was encouraged by another Pastor to try being a taxi driver. After a while, I accepted the encouragement and as I write I am still doing so.

I started to drive for a brother and did so for a few months and I returned the car to him at the beginning of 2002 due to circumstances beyond my control.

Losing our home!

In February of 2002, our church had three nights of prayer meeting, Monday through Wednesday, with the theme, "Call that which were not as if it were!" The Lord had directed me on the last night of the prayer meeting to call forth the things that were not as though they were, based on what the word of God says. It was also the first time I had used a theme for a prayer meeting. God has a sense of humour. On the second night, the Lord used me to call forth the things that were not as if they were: I bound what was supposed to be bound, I loosed what was to be loosed, I pulled down what ought to be pulled down. I loosed and called forth all the different currencies and called them forth into our hands. On Wednesday which was scheduled to be the last night of the prayer meeting at approximately eleven in the morning, our home was burnt down to the ground. All we saved were the clothes on our backs. It was a very sad day in our lives. But God was still in control. Our home was destroyed but our God, the great God of the universe was still alive and well and that meant we still had hope.

Look at how God is awesome. I was planning in the year 2003 to take my entire family to the United States because our visas would have expired that same year. However, we were unable to go anywhere as the visas were all burnt. I remember saying to God that I am cornered, but God had a reason for cornering us. We had a piece of land in Union Hall San Fernando, and we had done everything to have our home built the year before, but things did not work out. We had already made the down payment and signed the contract, but the house was not yet built. As soon as the house burnt down, two Saturdays later we began construction at our Union Hall property. We started with eight thousand dollars and God allowed us to build a house worth over three hundred thousand dollars because He is our provider.

Someone looked at me at that time and asked me if our house was burnt and I told them yes. Their response to me was, "Are you a Pastor?" "Pastor you must be committing some sin or something!" Another person wanted to see how we would catch ourselves. But God showed them. At this time, our home is not yet completed but it will soon be, and very soon. Before the house burned down, I had an appointment to do a week of meetings at a church in St. Vincent. After what had happened, I said, I now have reason to go. I had no clothes, no suitcase but God used someone to send fifty US dollars for me, with which I purchased three pairs of pants and five shirts. A sister brought some clothes for us from the US Virgin Islands, and she left the suitcase. That was my suitcase to travel to St. Vincent. My brother-in-law accompanied me to St. Vincent, and I saw the power of God in operation as never before. For the entire week, people were saved, healed, and delivered by the supernatural abundant power of God.

While I was away, our home was under construction and God used persons to bless us with the things we needed. Our home started with the encouragement of a good friend and brother. Two weeks prior, I was at the Housing Development Cooperation (H.D.C.) Office and they told me the office is closed but two weeks after when I went to the office, I just felt the leading of the Lord to tell the gentleman what had happened to us. There was a gentleman who had previously informed me they were not selling any house plans and I told him what had happened to us, and he walked to the filing cabinet drawer, pulled out the exact house plan that I needed and asked me if it was what I wanted. I replied in the affirmative. The house plan had a different person's name on it and I sat there watching him working on it and eventually I saw Wayne and Ann's name on that house plan. I did not receive the plan the same day due to additional work to be done on it, so I asked him for his contact number to contact him for an appropriate time to collect the plan. I told him that I would call him the next morning and he would just have to tell me that the persons to sign the plan were there and I would be already dressed and in Port of Spain to collect it the same day. I was excited to have the house plan in my hands. God worked it out and I went to Port of Spain and collected the plan to take it to the San Fernando Office. The following day, which was a Wednesday, God connected me to a former schoolteacher at the San Fernando Office and I collected the approval to commence building on the Friday.

I must say though, I remember laying on the bed one night where we were staying at the neighbours and felt something like a two and a half-inch hose pouring water on me. It was not a dream. I could hardly catch myself. It went on for like half hour and my hands were clearing the air because I felt like I was being stifled. After that experience, I heard a voice say to me, *anything you go to do within the next ten days you will get through with it,* and the next ten days, everything I put my hands to, I got through with it. Then I knew it was not ordinary what had happened to me but the anointed power of God was upon me like it was a new anointing I had received. I got up the said morning with new strength and when I started to move and get things done, my wife told me I was going and leaving her alone. My daughter Rachel who was I believe eleven years at that time, turned to her mother and said, "Mammy, daddy has to do what he has to do." I did not tell my daughter about the experience, but all I can say to it was, the Lord was speaking to her at that time. I can also say, I am now convinced that it was nobody else but the Lord who had spoken to me and I thank God that I got up and moved. It was new strength, new grace, bold faith, and the favour of God to back it up. I achieved some things in my life and family that I never experienced before.

But the enemy did not sit back and allow us to achieve just like that. He continued to attack us full force. After our home was burnt we saw some severe attacks by the enemy, However, it was also a time when we saw the greatness and faithfulness of God in a mighty way, which will always far outweigh the devil's plots to destroy. Remember I mentioned earlier, one person wanted to see how we would catch ourselves, what I didn't say was their choice of words were disturbing. We experienced folks in the fellowship whom we were looking forward to stand with us in this time of crisis walk out on us. Our church membership moved from forty members to seven members and my family additional. It was a big, big challenge to lead the fellowship. My family and I also looked out for my parents who also lost everything in the fire. At times my wife and I would be quarrelling, and it was really due to the frustration. It seemed like everything was locked up for us and I still had to officiate in all the services in our local church.

Trying times brought feelings of loneliness. However, we were not alone, God was always with us. There was also a Pastor friend and his wife, who were there for me and my family. In these times I believe God directed whom He desired to stand with us.

Some folks might say, 'we gave money', which we really appreciated. We received over fifty thousand dollars in gifts that God used people to bless us with. But friends, money is not all. At a time, the moral support was not there and it really put a beating on us. I want to emphasize that moral support is very important, especially in a time of crisis. So as you read, if you know about anyone going through a crisis, you may not have money, but moral support would do a lot for them. I also want to say, "Thank God," because even though at times we did not have moral support, God supported us in every situation.

What brought healing to my heart because I was really hurting, were the words of Bishop T.D. Jakes. A Pastor brought Bishop T.D. Jakes to Trinidad in 2003 for a conference, and my wife and I attended the conference. On the second day, he said something that brought healing to my hurting heart. He said, "Some leaders are lonely because God allows us to be lonely." He said, "Instead of building a relationship with God, we had built relationships with the people because we look for approval from the people and not from God." As he said those words I searched myself, repented, and something was done in my heart, and from that time I was healed of those hurts. So even though folks were distant when I expected them to stand with me, I realised it was the will of God what had happened and God turned the thing around for my good. Thank God for His strength. We lost our home in 2002 and in 2003 a lot of other things happened. My mother, who suffered from diabetes, one day felt her sugar gave a high reading, so she took medication to lower it, and instead of taking one tablet, she took two. This resulted in her sugar level dropping to the extreme and she had a mild stroke. I remember I was in prayer that morning when my wife brought the phone to me saying my brother-in-law is on the phone. Immediately, the Spirit of the Lord revealed to me, "Your mother is being attacked by a stroke." All he told me was that your mother is not well and I took authority against the spirit of stroke, rebuked it, pulled it down and cast it away from her physical body.

I continued to pray, took my wife and children to school, and then left to visit my mom. When I arrived at the home where they stayed at the time, my sister began to explain to me the condition of my mother. I thank God for His wisdom when he ministered to me to pray against the spirit of stroke. Thank God I was obedient. Mom was much better, although she could not even stand up in that same year.

I used to work taxi with a car from someone, and I used to make between three and four hundred dollars per day, but now, I was making about sixty dollars per day. After a while, I got discouraged and eventually returned the car to its owner. I told my wife all I needed was her approval to go and look for a car and she replied, "Go ahead." I got up one morning, got dressed, and went in search of a car without any money. In about one month's time, I had a brand new foreign used vehicle parked where I was staying. It did not happen just like that though. As a family, my parents, together with a sister spent three days in prayer and fasting, and on the second day, God came through. People were amazed. I must say though; I was led by God to return the previous car to its owner because I was just making sixty dollars per day. I made a step of faith and God came through for us.

In the same year of 2003, while driving a white B13, I saw a truck coming into the street on the wrong side of the road, the truck was facing the car, but I paid it no mind. The driver, just a few feet away was coming head on to the car which I was driving. I placed my two hands on the horn and began to honk the horn nonstop! The truck driver slammed a sudden brake, pushed his head outside the truck, and sincerely said, "I did not see you Nah." A woman in the car said in a loud tone of voice, "Driver you are a man of God, driver you are a man of God." That was sure death and I thank God for life and for saving our lives that day.

Another part of this eventful year was this: we wanted to go into our home, so I hired this gentleman to plaster four rooms for us. When he saw the job, he said he would charge twenty-five hundred dollars to plaster the four rooms, to which I agreed. I brought him to my home, he started the job and asked for some money. I gave him the sum of one thousand dollars. Within a space of two days, he asked for more money, so I gave him five hundred dollars. My wife and I began visiting the job site day after day and he was nowhere to be found, only the other workers were seen. When I could not take it anymore, I asked the remaining workers—two to be exact—to see the work they had done. I found that ninety-five percent of the work was completed. I then decided that I was not giving him any more money. The two gentlemen who were working begged me not to give him the money, but to give it to them instead, which I obliged and personally paid the men the balance. About two days later the gentleman called me inquiring if I had paid the men, I told him I did and he asked me for 'his money.' I then told him, *as far as I am concerned, I don't have any money for you.* His actual words were, "You please your heart I will please my mind," and he began to send threatening text time and time again to which I paid no mind. On December 3rd, 2003, I stood on a junction plying my taxi for hire and I observed the same gentleman passing by in a grey vehicle. He was gesturing at me with his hand as he passed, which I ignored. A few seconds later I saw four men coming towards me and they surrounded me by a vegetable stall on the junction. The men then began casting remarks like, "I want my money." One of the men said, "Take his money, take his car, take everything from him." They were brought by the worker I hired. While all this transpired, I did not panic nor was I scared in any way, I was just thinking. Suddenly, the gentleman who brought the men told them to kill me. One of the men who at the time was positioned right up in my face pulled out a ratchet knife with a dark brown handle. He opened the knife and was coming down to stab me. I looked at his face, but he continued. I looked around but it was as though I saw no one. I said to myself, *Well I would take one or two stabs, but today I have to fight, I am not running.* However, the knife was still coming down at my hand and when it was a few inches away, I saw a literal hand get between the knife and my hands and the voice said, "Rev, touch not the Lord's anointing and do His prophets no harm." The four men began to run. When I looked up it was a familiar face—a gentleman who I used to transport in my taxi, whether or not he had money. I thanked him for stepping in. That was the second attempt the enemy made to take me out but I thank God for Jesus.

I drive a taxi car but it's not my first choice. I really believe in my heart that God did not put me out there to just make money but there are lives God need to reach out to and He is using me to reach those people. There is a gentleman who visited our local church about two times. He came to me one day and shared some things with me. One of the things I appreciated about him was that he was honest about his struggle; he shared with me he had a substance abuse problem and just what it was, this he told me as we met, and he also declared he needed help with it. The first time we spoke he said, "Pastor Bedeau, I need to talk to you." I was going for lunch on that day and was not too concerned about talking at the time, but he insisted he wanted to speak to me, so he came into the car and I drove to the trace where I lived at the time. I told him I was going for lunch, and he began to relate his story to me. He confessed one of his incidents with the substance and admitted his actions, which has now left him indebted to someone. Additionally, the gentleman he owed came out from jail and wanted his money which he did not have. He had just started a job and the guy took his clothes and shoes so he could not go to work. I remember saying to him, *I don't have the money to give you, but I would do what I know best; that is pray.* The next week he returned with a good report, the guy did not come back. God had answered his request.

I saw him afterwards on different occasions. To me he needed money to buy foodstuff and somehow when I saw him from a distance I would say, *today, I am not giving him any money,* but after we were finished talking, I normally took out the money and gave it to him. There was a time I said, *Lord, I don't want to see this man again,* but when I missed him, I got worried and began asking for him.

I remember going to San Fernando one day to look for him but was unsuccessful. I kept looking until I found him and it was the same story, he wanted finance to get something to eat. There was a particular day while I sought out passengers on the junction where I usually would, he came and was speaking to me. In my mind I was saying, *this man doesn't realize that I'm out here to "hustle," time is money!* But he insisted on speaking with me even while my hands were up in the air as I asked potential passengers to travel, and he said something to me that really broke me that day. When he realized that I was not paying much attention to him, he said, "Pastor Bedeau, only you alone does listen to me!" I paused, put my hands down, turned to him, listened, prayed with him, encouraged him, and then gave him money to buy rice as he had asked after that conversation. I felt peace in my heart and the man went rejoicing.

I missed him for a while again and my concern about his whereabouts grew as I prayed for him. I started to work in a different area and was not coming down as regular as before. One day I decided to go to my old taxi area and work, it was after lunch. While passing through the village I saw him. I sounded my car horn, and he came into the car. He looked completely different; he had gained a little weight and he really looked good. His words were, "Pastor Bedeau, if I tell you something, would you believe?" He said, "Before I came down here, I prayed to see two persons." I asked him who, he responded, "You and my daughter, and look I see you." So, I asked him what the purpose was. He said that the time he was not around he was in a rehab centre, he was placed on a programme and got help, and he was then asked to teach the class at the centre. This day he was out to see his daughter and myself. The rehab centre was sending him to England to do another course and he was leaving the next day. He said, "Pastor, I would keep in contact with you," but after some months had passed, I did not hear from him and I questioned if he had set me up, but that was not the case. Two days later my phone rang, he called to say hello and that he was back in Trinidad and wanted to see me. We made arrangements and we met, and it was to officiate his wedding. I inquired whence he found his bride in such a short space of time, when he went to England. He replied, she was one of his friends while in Trinidad and they reconnected. They had already gotten married in England, and they needed to be married in Trinidad to get their papers processed. They were also already attending a church in England. I did their wedding and at present, they are happily married and living for the Lord. On Christmas day of 2010, they both called to thank me for the time I took with him. His wife said, they would never forget what God used me to do for him. All the honour and glory go to the Lord.

That's not all, there is this woman who travelled with me one day. As we spoke that day, she shared how she wanted to serve God and was living with a guy at the time, unmarried. I remember saying to her she needed to make a choice if she really wanted to serve God. It's either God or the man first; she had to decide who she would put first. About two years later she travelled with me again and the conversation began. I asked about how things were with her, and she replied, "Remember when you spoke to me that day, well, I left that guy, I am out of that relationship." I know God is great and mighty, but I was not actually shocked, rather moved by what God did in the life of the woman.

I also remember another woman who travelled with me, and when I dropped her off she told me that her daughter had a Rheumatism fever. I asked her if she would allow me to come to her home and pray for her daughter to which she replied in the affirmative. I went to her home, prayed for the young woman and God delivered her from the fever. Today the woman is a member of our local church. There are many other things I've seen God do by just walking in obedience to His call. It is said, the thing that you don't like, that's what God will call you into. Even though I am there, as a taxi driver, at present I know I would not be there for long again. In the meantime, I am trying to walk in obedience to God and allow Him to do what He wants to do in my life.

Two weeks after the fire, my first son Dwayne a.k.a. Silent Sah began to experience severe pains in his chest, to the extent that he had to be hospitalised on two occasions. The first time it happened, the pain was very severe. When we took him to the hospital there were no beds, so he laid on his mother. I left the ward around 12:30 am after waiting for over five hours for him to get a bed. My greatest hurt and pain on that morning was to leave my son sitting on a bench with his bag on his lap waiting to get a bed. Thank God when we returned the next morning, he had a bed. The second time when I took him to the hospital, we were waiting to see a doctor, and I remember telling him they would keep him in the hospital so long as it's chest pains. He said that he wanted to go home, and I asked him if he was trusting in God, or he just did not want to stay because I told him he would be warded. My son said to me that he decided to trust God. I took my son and we both left the hospital and I believe from that day he was healed of that pain. When the doctors did the X-ray, they said that it was a heart attack. But God be praised, He is our healer.

I must thank God for my children, all four of them, and also thank God for two sisters. Today my sons are Gospel Artistes because of an investment made in my life of a stereo set which they used to tape and sing songs. It was also used to practice the songs they learnt.

God has a way of raising up people. It was a time when all our singers had left the church. My children were not established singers, but I gave them the opportunity to go and represent the local church at a young age and God really used them. At present, they are established singers, Rachel is involved in the worship team and Joshua plays the Steelpan, the National Instrument. Thank God for his hands upon their lives Dwayne a.k.a. Silent Sah has already done one CD launch and the Lord has taken him to Grenada, Tobago, St. Vincent ministering the Word of God in song. Swayne has his own group by the name of Anointed One and they are doing well.

I must thank God for Glen and Joan for opening their doors to my family when we did not have a place to stay. The same night of the fire, they cleaned out their upstairs and allowed us to stay at no cost. We really appreciated their hospitality. God be praised! God always promised that He will make a way where there seems to be no way and He really did make a way.

Every time a church begins to grow in numbers, whether financially, in membership, or in spirituality, we have to be vigilant because the enemy launches severe attacks against that local church. That's why we must be consistent in prayer and be circumspect because the enemy always has a plan against us. After those two severe attacks against our local church, I decided to intensify prayer in our local church and God made a way so that it could happen.

The Spirit of the Lord spoke to me and told me to invite a missionary to our local church and lift an offering and give her every cent. I did not do it right away and the Spirit of the Lord came to me another time and repeated the same words. He also said, "Just as I use you to bless her, I would use someone to bless you." I immediately moved on it, made a phone call, and located her phone number, called her, and extended the invitation. She was ready to come the same Sunday and I pushed it back for the end of the month. The missionary came as planned, ministered, and we lifted the offering, and I gave to her every cent as God had instructed me to. About a month later, we were given an offer for office space to use by someone, and soon after that, a space to keep all our services. This took place, I believe, in the year 2009. However, I did not take up the offer at first. I prayed about it and sought God.

A message was then sent through my wife, inquiring if I did not want the church space. I was really pondering on it, it meant a change of location. Then the Spirit of the Lord spoke to me directly and reminded me that the Lord said He would use someone to bless me. Then I remembered and immediately messaged the person to accept the office space. I informed the brethren and even though I did not move with great faith, we made the transition. We moved in on old year's night. The new location was really a blessing. We could not keep all our services where we were before, but in our new location, we could keep all our services. I started a whole night prayer meeting in January 2010, and it has been very successful. We have seen some great results and changes take place in our local church. We also saw the revival of our mid-week services which we were having a serious challenge for the past four years to host. Thank God, after a while, we had consistent mid-week services for the year 2011. We even saw the birthing of a youth group in our local church, even though as I write our youth group is not functioning, but I am trusting God that our youth group will be revived very soon. We continued our prayer meeting in 2011 but reduced it to half night and God is doing a lot of great things through the ministry of prayer.

In the year 2010, Dwayne launched his first CD, not without some challenges. In 2011 he informed us that he wanted to get married. We did not take him seriously because he was not employed. But he was serious and set the date for boxing day 2011 and began to move forward to getting married. The time came close and him and his wife to be, were making arrangements. Christmas Eve day came and Silent Sah left San Fernando, I can't remember the time he left but it was after running about for the whole day, his destination was Diego Martin. On more than one occasion his sister and last brother told him not to go, but he still proceeded to make the long trip to Diego Martin. On his way back between 3:15 a.m. and 3:30 a.m. on Christmas morning, tired from the day before, he fell asleep and crashed into the back of a Toyota vehicle. The vehicle was thrown off the highway into a drain with the impact. We got the call around 3:30 a.m. All I heard that fateful morning was my wife bawling through sleep and wake. This was very different to deal with, so I called a good friend, and asked him to go to the scene of the accident. He did, and called and informed me, that even though there was a car in a drain, nobody died.

It took a great God to take a car over a drain, passing very close to a light pole without colliding with the pole. The two vehicles were in serious condition. We had to pay a wrecker to get the vehicle home. We were low on finance and my friend gave us one hundred dollars. We borrowed the remaining four hundred dollars and paid to bring the vehicle home early the next morning. The cost to repair the two vehicles was twenty-nine thousand, five hundred dollars and as stated before, we did not have the funds to do this. I went into a time of prayer and fasting for about one month, every half day I prayed and fasted asking God to provide the money for us to pay for the repairs of the vehicles, but the money was not coming.

I spoke to different persons telling of our plight, thinking they would say okay I would help you with so much and so much, but nobody responded to my call. The owners of both vehicles wanted to know how they would get their vehicles repaired. I was only making promises and more promises, and the money still was not coming. I decided to shield my wife and son from taking the calls; Dwayne was recently married, and my wife due to circumstances I felt should not be bothered with these calls. The calls continued to come in fast and furious and still I was not getting the money. I became more and more anxious as still no money came in. I went to the bank to apply for a loan but still no relief. The owners of the two vehicles were becoming more serious than ever, still no money. I kept seeking the Lord, asking Him to provide and He did.

I was lead in my spirit to ask a good minister friend, a prophet of the Lord, and I have to say that was really of the Lord because he did not disappoint me. I remember visiting and informing him of what had happened and the need we were in. He put me on to a businessman but kept repeating some powerful words to me, "Pastor Bedeau don't worry." Every time when I felt a little discouraged about the situation, I kept hearing these words in my head, "Pastor Bedeau don't worry." He also gave me a thousand dollars and repeated the same words, "Pastor Bedeau don't worry, don't worry." The prophet had a preaching appointment at my local church which he fulfilled. After the preaching, he lifted the offering on that day and I saw him taking money from a brief that he brought and was just putting it into the basket. There were cheques and cash. I saw him literally pulling out money from his brief, every corner of the brief that his hand could reach and where it had money, he took it out and sowed it into the offering basket. On that day he also sowed five thousand dollars from his ministry and said, "Pastor Bedeau this is for you, we came to bless you today." When I presented him with the love offering we lifted, he did not take it.

I thank God for him and his church; for that act of love towards me and my family and I will never forget what he had done for us. I really appreciated it greatly. To me, that was a crisis that we were in but God helped us at the right time. When the offering was counted, it accumulated to twelve thousand, three hundred dollars. Now it was not a nice position to be in not having any money at the present time. Bishop Garvin Garraway always said, pay yourself ten percent of your earnings. We put aside money, yes, but my wife's job became redundant, and my daughter got laid off from her job so I had to take up the slack financially. It was financially a challenge. Someone might say, well, your son made the accident so let him pay for the vehicle. But every family would help each other. For the information of the readers, I have since put a system in place for times of emergency and encourage readers to do the same. During that period, I experienced quite a lot! There were times when I was threatened, other times accused of not speaking the truth. But I was honest in my dealings with the two parties. I also believed God was allowing me and my family to learn a very hard but important lesson as well as my son. God never takes us through an experience without a purpose. He always has a purpose and a plan for our lives. Whether it's a bad or good situation, God has the power to bring good out of it and that He would continue to do. He is God all by Himself.

There was a businessman who played a critical role in all of this. I got an invitation to go and see the vehicle, which at that time was in Aranguez. He and a brother accompanied me to see the vehicle. I must say this, I know God and know He is able to protect and take care of us, and that is, at all times, and he also uses persons at times to accomplish his will. On that fateful evening, I thank God for the company of those two brothers. The distance I had to go was great and I did not know where I was going, I would swear those people were taking me to kill me, that's why I need to say thanks to these two brothers. They stood in the gap for me at that time and God knows how much I appreciated it. It's when we're going through a situation, we would see who is really for us. I did not know this brother. It was only on the recommendation of the prophet of the Lord this brother went with me and took the fight to the opponent on my behalf.

I had a few meetings with one party of the accident. It was most challenging and scary at times. At times, it looked like an unwise decision, but I was unaware that they were bringing four and five persons to meet with me. It was like David coming up against Goliath, but just like in those days where God allowed David to prevail, it was not just David, but it was the Father, Son, the Holy Ghost, and a host of Angels coming with David. God did the same for me and my family and at times even though I felt like I would be crushed to pieces, God did not allow us to be crushed, He has His way of working out things at the right time, "*...for in due season we shall reap, if we faint not." Galatians 6:9.* Meaning simply not to give up or give in.

I thank God for His wisdom because at times it was only the wisdom of God that took me through the fire, flood, and the flame. I literally felt at times that I would drown, burn up, or be consumed by the pressures of life but God be praised. He kept me by His power. The songwriter says, "His strength is made perfect when our strength is gone'; He'll carry us when we cannot carry on. Great is His power, the weak becomes strong His strength is perfect, His strength is perfect." We need to draw from God's strength every day because many of us feel we can make it on our own, but God will allow us to go thus far and bring us to ourselves, just as He allowed the Prodigal Son to come to himself.

I must mention some things about my good brother and fellow minister and father figure at times in the faith. I have lost a true friend, brother, and fellow minister when I did not expect it. I got to know this brother in the 90's. He gave me an invitation to attend a ministers' conference in St. Thomas. While contemplating attending, he convinced me to attend the conference and up to today, I have no regrets. I've always had the desire to go to Africa, I still have not gone to any of the nations of Africa as yet but still have that desire. In that conference, I met ministers from Africa, England, St. Croix, Jamaica, and other nations. I can recall, he was the first person who shared a prophetic word that God would have me as the man for the land.

He formed Repairers Ministry, and that brought together a wonderful group of ministers both nationally and internationally. He headed Repairers Ministry at that time with a vision that the brothers and myself all identified with. He felt that God was saying something to us, which was, we needed a forum to deliver and release what God was saying to us. He was truly not just a friend, brother, and father figure but he was an inspiration to me.

We began hosting free Gospel concerts and in 2008 we were hosting another of those free concerts at Harris Promenade, San Fernando. I remember when I went to drop off the invitation at my friend's church; I called him before, told him about the concert and he gave me the direction where to drop off the invitation, which I did. He did not tell me that he was in St. Vincent at the time. The concert was on the 31st of August 2008, a Saturday. My friend returned to the country that Saturday and he heard that the concert was still in progress, so he drove down to Harris Promenade just to give me the support. He was a person even though he may reach late, he would still give that support. He arrived around 11:30 p.m. and we hung out until about 12:35 a.m. I remember very clearly telling him I have some things to talk over with him, but due to the time, when we meet the next time we would talk.

We packed up our stuff and left the Promenade around 1:45 a.m. to prepare for service the same day. We had a wonderful service. I came home and was taking a much-needed rest when around 3:30 p.m. my phone rang. At the other end of the phone line was a Pastor friend with the sad news of my friend's passing.

It was the most shocking news I could receive. I still did my check by making a phone call hoping to get different news, but that phone call only confirmed what I had just heard. Questions why, how, what took place, I never got to talk over the things with my friend as I had told him. Could he not live? He was dead! Even though it still troubles me, I had to rest that case in the hands of the Lord.

A word of encouragement to my fellow ministers, *friends let's live our lives for God and nobody else. Let's be sold out to our King and give Him our all. It is a very challenging time that we are living in, but I believe the God of Israel is able to keep us in the most difficult of times as ministers. A word for us, don't give up, don't run away from the call of God upon our lives.*

I was in a situation as a minister when I experienced setbacks in making church rental payments and had nowhere to go. But I depended upon God, and He made a way for me. I remember that fateful morning I was worried about what to do, where to go, and God allowed me to meet with Pastor Joseph Thomas that morning. We started a conversation, and I told him what was taking place. He said to me, "Pastor Bedeau come use my church whether you have money or don't have money." It took a weight off my shoulder. I felt like a father that had nowhere to put his children! I thank God for using Pastor Thomas to help me in that area and pray God's richest blessing upon his life, family, and church.

When we did not have any money to pay the rent, I wrote out a cheque by faith hoping and trusting God that He will provide the money. But the money never came, and I was so ashamed and embarrassed not having the money to pay the church rent that I started to pass in the back streets. I wrote the cheque and was trusting that we would get the money to deposit in the bank. However, the cheque was returned but God be praised. The bible says in everything give God thanks. **I must thank you, thank you Lord, all the days of my life.**

I am taking this time off to thank God for our beautiful home that He blessed us with. I always had a dream to achieve our own home. When I was working regularly receiving a fortnight salary, we were unable to build a house, but God did it for us. God did it in the miraculous: it is one thing to get something and it's another to keep it. You have to put out more than what you used to achieve it in order to keep it. We faced our financial challenges to meet the monthly payments at times but depended on the God of Israel to see us through and He really did; He did by His power and might!

It's really a challenge at times to make the monthly payments. I am not telling anybody to do what I'm about to share with you. Due to circumstances, we had been having serious difficulty paying our mortgage over the years but due to God's mercy and grace, we still have our home.

This is not a boast, but my wife and daughter were not working, so I had to deal with all the bills, but God always came through for us. You might ask the question, "How on earth something like this can happen?" At times I asked the same question. It's not because of any good thing we had done. As the Apostle Paul says, but for the grace of God. It's only because of the grace and mercy of God that we kept our home. We had so many bills at that time to handle, but God held back the hands of the creditors and saved us from being embarrassed. I did not incur these bills intentionally. I prayed every day for God to hold back the hands of the creditors and trusted him that he would do it.

Family Matters

The year 2014 would go down as one of the most challenging years dealing with health. We were facing health issues with my dad and mom. It started from the beginning of the year when one of my parents was in the San Fernando General hospital. When my dad was out, my mom was in and so it continued for the entire year. Within that period my mom went into two diabetic comas, but God took care of her even in the comas and saved her life.

My dad had a semi-stroke that same year. God also kept him, and I thank God. That same year my dad was diagnosed with prostate cancer which had spread to his spine and the doctors gave him two years to live. As I write, he has lived one year and eight months, and if God spares his life to see September 22nd, 2016, he will be ninety years of age. My dad's life is in the hands of God.

When my sister Annie came to Trinidad in 2015 and decided to take my mom back with her to do a medical check-up, my mom told her one morning that she had something to tell her but not now. My sister insisted that mom tell her now and not later. When she broke the news, my mom had a mass in her breast. My sister told me about it and promised when she took her to the US she would let the doctors do a check on it. This was done in April 2015. The results revealed that mom had cancer in her breast. This was not good news to receive. In less than one year, both parents were diagnosed with cancer but thank God for His strength, grace, and mercy. God still has us standing on our two feet.

It did not end there. In the month of August 2015, my sister Annie called me from the States and informed me that my sister, Simonnette, was experiencing some pains on her right shoulder and to pray for her, which I did. She called back a few days after to find out if I was praying to which I responded, "Yes." She replied, the pain is more severe, so they took my little sister to the emergency department in the Hospital. They did their checks and came up with nothing. The doctor at the emergency also said to check with her doctor. The pain continued, and the following week she was taken back to the emergency but this time, after the doctors did their checks, they found that her organs were shutting down. I received the news in Trinidad early in September. Subsequently, I received another report that my sister had gone into a critical condition. They sent some pictures where my sister was hooked up on several machines. One for breathing, one for her pressure, one for her kidneys, and another for her lungs. I thank God for His strength! Every time my sisters and cousins called and gave me the report, it was that she was not looking good.

I told them that even in this, we have to trust God. On the 4th of September 2015, I left for America arriving on the 5th. My nephew took me up from the airport and drove straight to the hospital with me. When I entered the ward, the first thing I did was to rebuke the spirit of death from over my sister's life and continue to pray and trust God for her. For the next twenty days, my sisters and cousin were praying and interceding for my sister. We also had a few ministers come in and pray. We also had our Minister friends from Trinidad, my wife, and daughter who accompanied me to America praying and giving that moral support that was much needed at that time.

After about twenty days of intense, consistent prayer, she came out of the coma. Thank God for the doctors and nurses at the Hospital. There was one doctor in particular whom I can commend. While we were praying and interceding and declaring healing over our sister, they were giving us thumbs up and letting us know that God was hearing and answering our prayer. The doctors even told my brother-in-law and sister at one time that my sister was more dead than alive. When I saw my sister, it looked hopeless, but God made it possible and touched her body: her kidneys, lungs, and liver that were all failing, were restored back to normal. They even told us she was now better than us. I literally saw the dead raised back to life right before my eyes—a miracle I was longing to see happen for years. What an awesome God! It reminded me of Jairus, when Jesus told the father and mother don't be afraid only believe. Just as I pictured it in my mind, that as we continued to pray and believe God, one day we would go to that hospital and the tubes would be out of my sister's throat, lungs, kidneys and the other parts of her body, God did it the exact way. One day we went to visit her, and one tube was taken out. The following day, another tube was removed and the next day another. We give God the praise. When I left America on the 28th of September 2015, my sister was out of the hospital and she called for a thanksgiving and gave God the praise for keeping her. Even as I visited the United States this year April, my sister was facing another challenge with her health where she was diagnosed with cancer. But God be praised, she is taking some treatment and responding pretty well. God will not give us more than we can bear. ***Though he slay me, (kill me) yet will I trust in him: but I will maintain mine own ways before Him,*** **Job 13:15 (KJV).**

I give God the praise for birthing our first ministry in Brooklyn New York on May 1st, 2016 and continue to covet your prayer as we pray for the leaders together with their two beautiful children. There was a series of events that occurred after the word of the Lord was spoken over the ministry in our first Ordination Service. When the ministry was established in 1999, we invited a Pastor as our speaker for that meeting. On that same day we also ordained two elders and three ministers. There was a powerful move of God that day! In the meeting the word that God used the Pastor to speak was that God would use me to establish churches in Brooklyn, Washington D.C. and Canada.

On the 27th of February 2014, we had to move from the building that we were occupying due to circumstances beyond our control. On the 30th of March that same year, in our Sunday Morning Service, we had to deal with a situation in our service that was not so nice. Since 2012 to 2014 our worship team has been under attack by the enemy. Nevertheless, in all this God brought us out victorious.

In the month of February, my dad fell during the wee hours of the morning, cutting below his eye. When we took him to the hospital, the CT scan was done, and the doctors said it was a mild stroke. He spent four days in the hospital. A few months later, my eldest sister who was taking care of dad and mom, (my dad was now out of hospital and my mom was now hospitalised) had a pot on the stove and went to take a shower. She remembered the stove and came out of the bathroom to turn off the burner. In the hassle, she slipped and fell on the tile floor hitting her head and hip against the wall. This happened on the 14th of April 2014. On April 15th, 2014, returning from bible study at Fyzabad around 9:15 p.m. I received a call from her that she could not move due to the fall from the previous day, and she was calling the ambulance to take her to the emergency room because she was experiencing severe pains. I drove up to my parents' where my sister was waiting until the ambulance arrived and assisted her into the ambulance for the Hospital.

I give Jehovah God all the praise, glory and honour, for He said in His word, **"Be careful for nothing; but in everything by prayer and supplication with thanksgiving let your requests be made known unto God." Philippians. 4:6 (KJV).** I visited my sister at the hospital on the 16th of April 2014 to be greeted with the news that after the doctors did the x-ray of her back and hip the result was that her back was fractured. I still gave God praise because even though her back was fractured she was not dead but alive. I then took over making sure my dad and mom had something to eat and I visited her and my mom at the hospital.

I must thank God for the persons who gave us a great deal of help in our time of need. They made sure my dad had something to eat and even took time to wash his clothes. I continue to give God praise. Why? Because He is wise, never makes a mistake and He is God all by Himself.

While checking on my parents, my sister Annie who lives in the United States called and informed me that after hearing the news about Brenda's fall and condition, she and Brenda's daughter, could not sleep but started to pray around four in the morning. They were praying and calling all the family's names. She said she called her son and told him to be careful. He called her back about two and a half hours later and asked her, "Mammy what is the last thing you told me?" She reminded him she said to be careful. He then gave her a true story. He told her he was driving his wife's truck, and he opened the front door to the driver's seat and did not have a chance to close the door, when a car driven by a female driver knocked the entire door off the vehicle. Thank God for the prayer of his mother. Who knows what would have been the outcome, it could have been worse. When I heard that, I was convinced my family was under attack by the enemy.

God's word said, He will not give us more than we can bear. It's not over until God say it's over! Since my mom came out of the hospital, I visited every day. Easter Monday was the only day I did not. Feeling a bit tired, I decided to visit them on the Tuesday Morning. On that morning 22nd April 2014, I was returning from taking my wife to work, when I received a phone call around 7:08 a.m. from a sister. She was crying and said to me, "Pastor Wayne, I went to check on your mom and she is in a worse condition than the last time, I don't know what to do." I remember telling her to keep calm and I would call the ambulance. I was in a bit of shock that I had the ambulance's number on my phone and could not find it! I had to compose myself and after a while I found it. The ambulance service responded in record time. When I broke the news to my daughter she began to cry. I went back to my wife's job, took her up and we all headed to the emergency department at the Hospital. Thank God for my wife, daughter, nephew Kevon, friend Joy and even Silent Sah who gave their moral support on that day arriving at the hospital. When we inquired about my mom, the doctors were trying to resuscitate her because she was in a diabetic coma. I would not go into the room at that time, so my wife went in and she was informing us what was taking place inside. I sat and thought to myself, *Today I am losing my mom*, so, outside I was prepared to accept any news, but was also trusting God for the best. My wife then came out from the room and said, "Wayne your mother says she wants to see you." I said to myself, *if she tells me things like, Wayne take care of your father for me, I love you all, well she is going. But if I hear a different conversation she isn't going anywhere.*

I was very unsettled upon entering the room. I walked to my mom and said, *Tanty, how you going?* She replied, "Boy ah good, but not so good." She looked drowsy and pale, and her eyes looked weak. I laid my hand upon her head and began to pray for her. By the evening she was in a far better condition than when she went in. I continue to give God the praise.

My sister Annie arrived in Trinidad on March 3rd, 2014, to give us some much-needed help. I thank God also for my other sister, Bernadette, who arrived sometime around the 28th of February 2014 to also give some support to us. After a period, we had to move our dad from the family home and place him in a home for the elderly due to his illness, Alzheimer disease, in February 2015. It was a difficult decision for me to move my dad from the home that he built and spent many years in. My mom and sister Brenda at that time could not cope with him anymore. It was a challenging time not just for me but for the entire family. I did not have the strength at that time to take him out from his home, but with the help of my sister Bernadette we had to do it to preserve my mom and sister.

My dad, due to his illness, at times, was very aggressive with my mom and our sister before we took him to the home for the aged. She took care of our dad, and the family was pleased with the care given to our dad. Every time we visited, dad was clean and smelling good. She really went beyond the call of duty to make our dad comfortable, and for those who know Mr Robert John Bedeau knows he could be a handful at times. I remember one day I went to visit my dad and I asked the caretaker if she wanted help with the wheel chair, and she responded, "No, if you are not here, I have to get the wheel chair inside." I simply backed off and allowed her to do her thing and just smiled. I really admire the staff at this home for their commitment in taking care of the elderly. God richly bless you all. I don't know about my sister, but my biggest challenge was when I visited my dad and he would ask me, "When are you taking me home?" I felt like I was tearing up on the inside, but God continued to give me the strength and courage to face it. Even though at times I had to encourage myself, at the end I made it.

Some memories about my dad: there were days we would visit, and we would have to remind him who we were, and there were days he would remind us who we were. For the two years and two months my dad spent in the home there was a different bonding that took place. When I arrived, he would ask, "Is that my son, Pastor Wayne Bedeau?" and was always glad when we arrived to visit him. At age ninety he would confess to his wife how lovely she was and he still loves her. My dad also shared the sentiments to me of how much he loved me. There was one time after my mom returned from a trip to the US he pointed out to her that she had dropped some weight, but he bellowed out, "Your husband loves you still girl!"

I remember when I returned from the States last year November and visited him, I saw something that I did not see for two years and more. My dad got up and was coming to the edge of the bed. I was looking and saying I am seeing something different here today because he came right to the edge of the bed and was sitting up. He looked bright, fresh, and young and he said to me, "Pastor Wayne Bedeau how are you looking good so, your wife taking good care of you boy!" He repeated that about five times. We had a very lengthy conversation and after about an hour, I prayed with him and left. That was on the 23rd of November 2016, and that's the last time I spoke to him and saw him alive. I was satisfied in my heart that I had at least spent some time with my dad. He would always bless me. In his early life he cursed us but in his latter days he would always bless his children.

On the morning of the 13th day of December, I received a call from the care-taker stating, dad did not have a good night. That day I was fasting and decided I was not leaving the house. Often, he would have some of those days and nights when he would tell us that he would not make it and I would encourage him that you would live and not die. Then he would confess, I would live and not die. So I informed her that I would visit him the next day, but around 12:40 p.m. that said day, I received a call from my sister Brenda saying that she also got a call informing her that daddy is not feeling well, however, she was unable to go to the home right away, so I told her I will go. I got up, took a bath and headed to do some business then proceeded to check my dad. I got another call from my sister around

1:00 p.m. saying, "Wayne where are you?" and with the sad news that she just received a call that dad just passed away.

I've always heard people talk about when their loved ones die how they feel something go up and down in their stomach, I could say I have experienced that feeling but for a short while. If I say I was not prepared, I would be lying. The year 2014 when my dad and mom were in and out of the hospital that was preparation time. The prophetic word that my family and I received from the prophet of God prepared us for this time in our lives. I Thank God that He strengthened me so I could move around and get all the papers to organise my dad's burial and also for giving me the courage to share a powerful word in my dad's home going service on the 20th of December 2016.

One day before my second son Swayne's birthday, as I write, I am still trying to come to terms with the loss of my dad. Even though I know the word of God says to be absent from the body is to be present with the Lord and I know he is in a better place because he had a relationship with God and knew God, I still struggle. I was unable to see the grave being covered because I had left to collect some food for after the funeral. I wanted to be there till the end but could not be there. I walked out from my home the following Friday and took a taxi to the cemetery to look at the grave and I took some pictures with my phone just to bring closure. Doing that brought a peace in my heart.

As I close this chapter, I must thank Jehovah God for my dad and for the impact he made in my life. He did not leave money, land or house but he left a legacy of righteousness, holiness and faithfulness towards God, community and family life. A word of advice for all husbands: stay faithful to one wife and take care of your family. There are some challenges that we still face: my mom is still battling cancer; my sister also has a terminal illness, but we continue to intercede on their behalf and trust God for total healing of their physical bodies. We continue to serve a God of miracles, might and power.

God has been faithful to me!

God continues to be faithful to me!

He IS FAITHFUL!!

GOD of MIRACLES, MIGHT, AND POWER—I praise You for Your FAITHFULNESS TO ME!

www.ingramcontent.com/pod-product-compliance
Lightning Source LLC
LaVergne TN
LVHW041545070526
838199LV00046B/1834